ROUTLEDGE LIBRARY EDITIONS: LITERACY

Volume 10

READING TO LEARN

READING TO LEARN

SHEILA HARRI-AUGSTEIN, MICHAEL SMITH
AND LAURIE THOMAS

LONDON AND NEW YORK

First published in 1982 by Methuen

This edition first published in 2018
by Routledge
2 Park Square, Milton Park, Abingdon, Oxon OX14 4RN

and by Routledge
711 Third Avenue, New York, NY 10017

Routledge is an imprint of the Taylor & Francis Group, an informa business

© 1982 Sheila Harri-Augstein, Michael Smith and Laurie Thomas

All rights reserved. No part of this book may be reprinted or reproduced or utilised in any form or by any electronic, mechanical, or other means, now known or hereafter invented, including photocopying and recording, or in any information storage or retrieval system, without permission in writing from the publishers.

Trademark notice: Product or corporate names may be trademarks or registered trademarks, and are used only for identification and explanation without intent to infringe.

British Library Cataloguing in Publication Data
A catalogue record for this book is available from the British Library

ISBN: 978-1-138-55984-4 (Set)
ISBN: 978-0-203-70159-1 (Set) (ebk)
ISBN: 978-0-8153-7272-1 (Volume 10) (hbk)
ISBN: 978-1-351-23678-2 (Volume 10) (ebk)

Publisher's Note
The publisher has gone to great lengths to ensure the quality of this reprint but points out that some imperfections in the original copies may be apparent.

Disclaimer
The publisher has made every effort to trace copyright holders and would welcome correspondence from those they have been unable to trace.

Reading to Learn

SHEILA HARRI-AUGSTEIN
MICHAEL SMITH AND
LAURIE THOMAS

METHUEN
LONDON AND NEW YORK

First published in 1982 by
Methuen & Co. Ltd
11 New Fetter Lane, London EC4P 4EE
Published in the USA by
Methuen & Co.
in association with Methuen, Inc.
733 Third Avenue, New York, NY 10017

© 1982 Sheila Harri-Augstein, Michael Smith and Laurie Thomas

Printed in Great Britain by
J. W. Arrowsmith Ltd., Bristol

All rights reserved. No part of this book may be
reprinted or reproduced or utilized in any form
or by any electronic, mechanical or other means,
now known or hereafter invented, including
photocopying and recording, or in any information
storage or retrieval system, without permission
in writing from the publishers

British Library Cataloguing in Publication Data
Harri-Augstein, Sheila
Reading to learn.
1. Reading
I. Title   II. Smith, Michael
III. Thomas, Laurie
428.4'3   LB1050

ISBN 0-416-72660-7

Library of Congress Cataloging in Publication Data

Harri-Augstein, E. Sheila.
Reading to learn.

1. Reading. I. Smith, Michael. II. Thomas,
Laurie F. III. Title.
LB1050.H325   428.4   82-7864
ISBN 0-416-72660-7 (pbk.) AACR2

Contents

	List of figures	vi
	List of activities	vii
	Acknowledgement	vii
	Foreword	viii
	User guide to this book: a flow diagram of the chapters	xii
1	The approach: an overview	1
2	Reading tactics and reading strategies	13
3	Reading purposes	34
4	Reading for meaning	51
5	Meaning and strategy	68
6	Reading outcomes	75
7	Becoming a competent reader: putting it together	87
	Epilogue Notes for the tutor	109

Figures

1.1	The process of reading to learn	9
1.2	The hierarchical organisation of units of meaning	12
2.1	A simplified version of a record obtained on the reading recorder	15
2.2	Five basic patterns of reading	17
2.3	A reading strategy found to be effective for answering multiple-choice questions	20
2.4	A reading strategy found to be effective for summarising a difficult text	21
2.5	Tracking your reading	22
4.1	Using a flow diagram to map meaning	60
4.2	Mapping the flow of meaning at a more detailed level	61
5.1	(a) Overall sentence read	70
	(b) Tactic 1 – a smooth read	70
	(c) Tactic 2 – an item read	71
	(d) Tactic 3 – a search read	72
	(e) Tactic 4 – a smooth read	72
6.1	Diagrammatic illustration of a meaning net	81
6.2	How to display a reading outcome in structured form	82
6.3	Lisa's meaning net before review	85
6.4	Lisa's meaning net after review	86
7.1	Students' use and misuse of reading skills	103
7.2	An algorithm for process-conversations with texts	108

Activities

1.1	Developing an awareness of the reading to learn procedure	10
2.1	Tracking your own reading	21
2.2	Recording your reading tactics	26
3.1	Constructing a purpose hierarchy	37
3.2	Reading purposes and comprehension	39
3.3	Using the purpose taxonomy to classify comprehension skills	41
3.4	Using command words to relate purpose to text	48
4.1	Mapping meaning	51
4.2	Identifying signpost phrases	54
4.3	Using context cues to find meanings	54
4.4	Classifying context cues	57
4.5	Mapping the meaning of a paragraph by means of a flow diagram	63
6.1	Checking on reading outcomes	77
6.2	Showing reading outcome in 'structure of meaning' form	83
6.3	Using a meaning net to review outcome	86
7.1	Reading to learn: the process as a whole	89

Acknowledgement

The authors and publishers would like to thank the President and Fellows of Harvard College for permission to reproduce William G. Perry, 'Students' Use and Misuse of Reading Skills: A report to a Faculty', *Harvard Educational Review*, *29*, 193–200 (© 1959 by President and Fellows of Harvard College).

Foreword

Reading to learn

Reading to learn is something that we nearly all do. The point of teaching reading in school is partly to develop the ability to learn from books. One learns to read in order to read to learn. Of course, there are many other reasons for reading; but reading to learn enters so deeply into our general intellectual growth that it is a crucially important skill to acquire.

In this book we are not really concerned with young children's reading patterns, although some of the techniques described later have in fact been tried out fairly extensively with primary school children and seem to have proved helpful. Our concern is rather with the new kinds of demand on our reading ability made by the reading we undertake for A level, or in college, or at university; or, indeed, at work.

It might be thought that if someone has reached this level then their reading skills can be taken for granted. We can only say that is not our experience. Nor, it appears, is it the experience of lecturers in an increasing number of colleges and universities, many of whom are arranging reading courses for their students. There is considerable support, not least among students themselves, for the view that the kind of demand upon reading ability made by higher education requires new skills, new strategies, a new approach altogether.

Even if that were not true, there might still be a case for looking at our reading skills. Donald Bligh, in his book *What's the Use of Lectures*, puts the point well:

> If we imagine a student on a three-year course who reads 11 hours per week during ten-week terms but never during vacations nor at any time in the rest of his life, he would need to make less than 3% improvement in reading efficiency after 30

Foreword ix

hours' tuition before we could say that the time training him to read faster was not saved by increased efficiency.

Bligh adds the comment 'The failure of most colleges to provide training in reading to learn is, in my opinion, little short of a disgrace.'

It is a failure which many institutions are seeking to remedy. What is often lacking, however, is adequate materials for such training. The object of this book is to provide such materials.

Who is the book for?

The book, then, is for people who already possess fundamental reading skills but who are being obliged to use them in situations which make new, more complex demands on them. Many of these people will be students at colleges, polytechnics and universities making the difficult transition from sub A level work to work at degree, diploma or certificate level. An increasing proportion of these will be relatively mature people returning to study after a break and understandably feeling diffident about the capability of their somewhat rusty learning skills. Some may not be students at all but just people anxious to improve their reading ability for perfectly good reasons of their own. The approach developed in this book has been tried out with many people of this sort, with undergraduates of many disciplines, including engineers, sociologists, biologists, and chemists, with students of art, education, architecture and music, with sixth formers and with adults working in a variety of occupations. It is the outcome of a great deal of work in the field, stretching now over ten years.

How to use the book

The book is addressed directly to the individual reader. This is deliberate. We shall argue later that unless the individual takes responsibility for his own reading, it will not improve. However, in compiling this book we have had in mind not so much the lone reader as a course for a group, such as Bligh envisages and so many institutions are beginning to provide. The book is written as a self-tutoring workbook and so should be suitable for an individual

x *Reading to Learn*

working alone. However, we assume that the reader will normally be part of a group, and so we have built in some exercises which are best performed in pairs. There is a real pedagogic advantage in this since another person can often provide the monitoring of reading performance which is hard to do for oneself. Nevertheless, having someone else to work with is not essential, and such exercises can be omitted. The reader is not expected to work religiously through all the exercises we have included. This is a workbook not a programmed text. We have tried to provide an abundance of material and the learner (or tutor) is expected to select according to his perception of his needs.

What we have provided is a number of exercises together with an interleaving commentary. This material should not, definitely not, be read straight through as if it were an ordinary book. The reader should read the relevant part of the commentary, think about the points made, and then turn to the exercises both for help in understanding the points and for practice in the techniques suggested. The reader should then re-read the commentary asking questions about every point of difficulty. The text may not answer them, or the answer may not become clear until later in the book, but if you are asking the questions right from the start you will be beginning to emancipate yourself from print, and from us, and starting to assume responsibility for your reading performance. Another point: you will have to add material of your own, taken from your own reading. That will be good. The book is only a point of departure. If you seriously intend to alter and improve your reading you will need to become more aware of your reading performance whenever you read. What you learn from the book has to be applied outside it. That is part of what we mean by the reader taking responsibility for his own performance. Confining yourself to the book, and trying to improve your skill only when you are reading the book, is not enough.

How much time, then, should the reader be expecting to spend? We have taken as a basis the notion of a course extending over fifteen two-hour sessions, i.e. thirty hours in all. This is a fairly standard length for courses in advanced reading techniques. It represents a considerable investment in time and energy on the part of the reader, but if he or she is genuinely seeking a permanent improvement in reading efficiency such a commitment is necessary. After all, as Bligh points out, an investment on that scale is likely to pay for itself reasonably quickly given even a modest improvement in reading efficiency. Our results indicate that people can develop their reading competence very significantly given the commitment we suggest. In fact we have found it possible to convey the general lines of the approach effectively in six two-hour sessions. The more time available for practice and consolidation, however, the better.

Learning to learn

Finally, let us briefly point forwards to skills other than reading which are important for intellectual growth. In this book we are concerned with helping people to improve their abilities to use the printed media as resource for learning. We have developed a model of the process (Chapter 1 and Fig. 1.1) and a battery of techniques for raising awareness and encouraging reflection and review of how, why and what people learn by reading. We have successfully applied this approach to writing, listening and discussion as learning skills. For example, the flow diagram and structures of meaning techniques can be usefully applied to help people improve their essays, project work, personal notes and examination answers. Again, listening effectively in lectures and participation in seminars and tutorials can be considerably improved by the adoption of a purpose – strategy – outcome – review approach. Readers who take on the responsibility for developing their reading to learn skills might usefully consider how they can apply this approach to other areas of learning skill.

User guide to this workbook: a flow diagram of the chapters

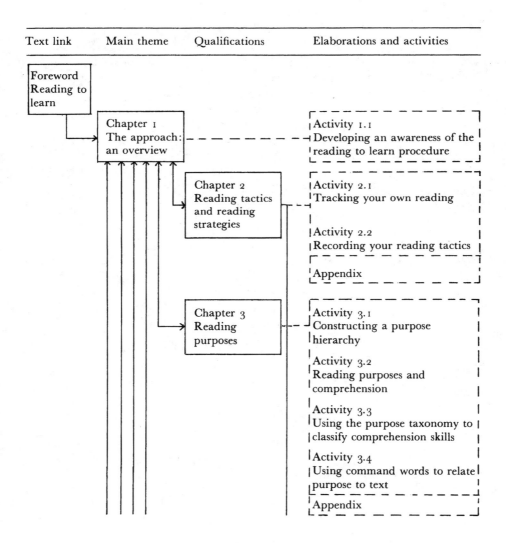

User guide to this workbook—*continued*

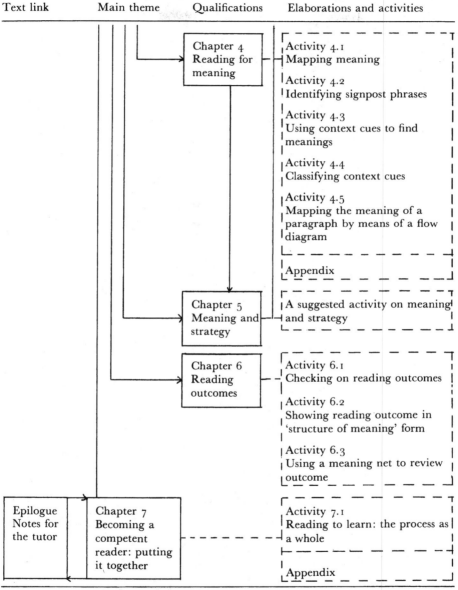

Text link	Main theme	Qualifications	Elaborations and activities
		Chapter 4 Reading for meaning	Activity 4.1 Mapping meaning
			Activity 4.2 Identifying signpost phrases
			Activity 4.3 Using context cues to find meanings
			Activity 4.4 Classifying context cues
			Activity 4.5 Mapping the meaning of a paragraph by means of a flow diagram
			Appendix
		Chapter 5 Meaning and strategy	A suggested activity on meaning and strategy
		Chapter 6 Reading outcomes	Activity 6.1 Checking on reading outcomes
			Activity 6.2 Showing reading outcome in 'structure of meaning' form
			Activity 6.3 Using a meaning net to review outcome
Epilogue Notes for the tutor		Chapter 7 Becoming a competent reader: putting it together	Activity 7.1 Reading to learn: the process as a whole
			Appendix

Note. The flow diagram technique for text analysis is described in detail in Chapter 4.

I
The approach: an overview

Introduction

In this chapter we set out our approach in general terms. We introduce the reader to a number of ideas which will be more fully developed in later chapters. Our intention here is merely to give the reader a provisional working framework within which to fit particular ideas as they come up. We begin by asking exactly what is going on when a person is reading. We suggest that as you read you predict meanings and check against textual cues whether they are correct or not. A sort of conversation goes on with yourself though you are probably not aware of it. The 'conversation' is mostly concerned with the meaning of the text, i.e. with what we call 'product' or 'content'. What is needed, we argue, is to develop techniques for having a 'conversation' about *process*, about the *ways* you read. We then go on to sketch a preliminary language for that conversation by suggesting that we talk about reading in terms of *purpose, strategy, outcome* and *review*.

What is going on when a person is reading something?

Opinions differ, but one view which we find attractive has been gaining ground in recent years. This sees reading as essentially a continuing series of predictions about the text. Here, for instance, is a record of a relatively proficient young reader reading a passage aloud. A stroke through a word with a word written in above indicates a mispronunciation or substitution. A curved arrow indicates a repetition:

> hoped a
> So education it was! I ~~opened the~~ dictionary and picked out a word
>   s   Ph
>   that sounded good. Phil/oso/phi/cal I yelled. Might as well study
> what it means   1. Phizo 2. Phiso-soophical
> ~~word-meanings~~ first. ~~Philosophical~~: 'showing calmness and
>   his
> courage in ~~the~~ face of ill fortune'.

2 Reading to learn

We see that in the second sentence the reader substituted 'hoped' for 'opened' and 'a' for 'the'; and he had to have several tries at the word 'philosophical' in the third sentence, repeating it syllable by syllable. What is interesting is that the substitutions are nearly all perfectly sensible ones; they accord, that is, with what the reader could expect the next word to be having read so far. In the fourth sentence, for example, it looks as if the child registered the 'w' of the word after 'study' and then guessed ahead to what followed. Actually, the guess was quite a good one. 'What it means' fits in perfectly well with the sense. To take another example: in the second sentence it looks as if the child correctly identified the word 'sound' but predicted the ending wrongly. 'Sounds' would, however, have been correct grammatically and would also have made sense.

Since the predictions are not random but fit in with the requirements of sense and grammar it seems likely that they are made as part of a pattern of continuing response to cues in the text. Cues encountered *after* prediction help the reader to check whether the prediction was correct. In the second sentence, for instance, it might be that the reader responded to the 'o' sign in 'opened' but predicted – wrongly – the word 'hoped'. When he had read a little further he saw that 'hoped' would not do; it would not fit in with the rest of the sentence. Accordingly, he abandoned the prediction, went back and made another, correct, one.

It seems that as the reader reads he or she is predicting meanings that will be symbolised by the words on the page. The reader's eyes scan the words to discover whether they are compatible with his or her expectations. This scanning process continues evenly unless the reader's expectations are not met. If that happens the process falters. A mismatch occurs between expectation and meaning. Such a mismatch can occur for many reasons. The reader may have predicted wrongly the meaning of a single word or phrase, or perhaps the whole drift of his expectation is wrong. What then happens is that he has to search the text more carefully for cues which will help him to find the right meaning. He then returns to the high-speed scanning which characterises the normal flow of reading.

Obviously this is a very curtailed and over-simplified description of a highly complex process. The example was taken from an article by Goodman and the reader may wish to refer to his writings for a more detailed account. There are other views of the reading process

The approach: an overview 3

but the predictive model which we develop later in the chapter seems to us especially helpful for thinking about the reading behaviour of experienced readers, of undergraduates or students taking A level, whose reading skills are already well advanced.

For one thing, the process of prediction, of attributing meaning to the marks on the page, depends to a great extent on the use the reader is able to make of context, both the context provided by the text and the wider context provided by the reader's own experience, knowledge, interests and purposes. An experienced reader brings a great deal to the act of reading. Such a reader has, indeed, a considerable advantage over younger, less experienced readers, and an approach to reading which starts from that fact is likely to prove particularly fruitful for present purposes.

Another feature of the approach which attracts us is that it does not present reading as a passive process of deriving meaning from the text. Instead, it sees the reader as constantly taking initiatives, as continually proposing meanings to the text. We shall argue that it is this reader initiative which opens up the possibility of improving one's reading ability. If one can nurture the process of reader initiative then one can operate consciously upon one's reading patterns. The first thing we need to do, then, is to become more aware of ourselves as readers.

Reading self-awareness

If we ask someone about the way they read they will not reply, of course, in terms anything like those we have put forward above. Usually people volunteer statements like the following:

I read word by word.

I read from the beginning to the end.

I can read all right, but I cannot remember afterwards what I've just read.

I can't concentrate for long. My mind wanders.

Surprisingly often replies reveal personal superstitions about reading:

I need to smoke.

4   *Reading to learn*

I must be alone.

I must have the radio on.

Such knowledge is at the level of sympathetic magic. Even when the replies are more to the point there is usually very little awareness of their implications.

I always read the same way.

I make different sense from an article if I read it again.

I read the important bits usually.

People's knowledge of the way they read tends to be fragmented. They have several bits of information but they do not know how to bring the bits together into a coherent explanation. They lack, in our terminology, the tools for a satisfactory conversation about reading.

The reading conversations

Goodman describes reading as a kind of 'psycholinguistic guessing game'. Efficient reading, in his view, results from skill in selecting the fewest and most productive cues necessary to produce guesses which are right first time. We prefer to think of reading as a kind of conversation between the reader and the text. The reader puts questions, as it were, to the text and gets answers (what we have called 'cues'). In the light of these he puts further questions, and so on.

For most of the time this 'conversation' is inaudible. It goes on below the level of consciousness. At times, however, we become aware of it. This is usually when we are running into difficulties, when mismatch is occurring between expectations and meaning. We sometimes catch ourselves saying to ourselves things like 'What on earth is he talking about?', 'Where have I got to?', 'Hallo, I've missed something' or 'I'm completely lost. I shall have to go back and start again'. It is then that the conversation becomes audible. Significantly, it is when mismatch is occurring. When successful matching is being experienced our interrogation of the text continues at the unconscious level. There is no need to bring the process into the foreground of our consciousness.

Different people converse with the text differently. Some stay

The approach: an overview 5

very close to the words on the page; others take off imaginatively from the words, interpreting, criticising, analysing and extrapolating. The former represents a kind of comprehension which is 'literal' (i.e. as written in the text). The latter represents higher levels of comprehension (i.e. as interpreted by the reader). Actually, the reader is always doing both to some extent. You cannot take off imaginatively unless you have first understood the words at some kind of literal level. However, we have found in practice that people often tend to one extreme or the other. They are either over-conformist as readers (and don't take off critically enough) or undisciplined as readers (and don't pay sufficient regard to what the text actually contains). The balance between these is important, especially for advanced readers. The kind of reading required in further or higher education places considerable emphasis on both.

The conversation that we have been so far concerned with has been to do with meaning, with the content of the text. But there is another kind of conversation which from our point of view is equally important, and that is to do not with what is read but with how it is read. We call this a 'process' conversation as opposed to a 'content' conversation. It is concerned not with meaning but with the mechanics of our reading, with the strategies we employ and with appraisal of their effectiveness. If we are an advanced reader our ability to hold a content conversation with a text is usually pretty well developed. Not so our ability to hold a process conversation. It is precisely this kind of conversation that is at issue when we are seeking to develop our reading ability to meet the new demands being placed upon us by studying at a higher level. Before we can have a conversation about process, however, we need some kind of language for conducting that conversation.

Some preliminary vocabulary for a process conversation

We would like to introduce at this point four terms which we shall use a great deal later on. They are *purpose, strategy, outcome* and *review.*

PURPOSE

People read for different purposes. Sometimes they are reading in

6 *Reading to learn*

order to locate a single item of information ('What was that name?'); sometimes they are reading to acquire several items of a fairly factual nature; sometimes the facts do not matter much but the general argument does, and the reader is trying to grasp a theory. There are, we shall find, very many different purposes for reading.

Now purpose is very important to reading. First, we shall see that the way you read, your reading strategy, can and should vary according to purpose. If your purpose is to locate a single item an appropriate strategy, for instance, is to scan the text quickly. If you are reading to acquire several items scanning will not do. In order to develop your reading, therefore, the first thing you have to do is to be very precise about your reading purpose. Secondly, in order to be able to measure how effective your reading is (and that is certainly essential if you want to improve it) you have to check it against something, and that can only be purpose.

Purpose may seem an easy concept to grasp, and the tendency is to pass quickly over it. In fact, it is in many ways the most difficult of our terms and we shall find that the chapter devoted to it is by no means a simple one. Many problems in the development of advanced reading skills begin here.

STRATEGY

Strategy is the way in which the reader approaches the text. The first thing to understand is that the text may be approached in various ways, according to one's reading purpose: that is, there is more than one strategy available to the reader. Thus the person who replied that he always reads in the same way, whatever the text and whatever the purpose, is unlikely to be reading well. At the very least he is restricting himself severely in the way he approaches the text. The mark of good reading is to vary one's strategy appropriately. To do that it helps to know what strategies are available. That will be the subject of our next chapter. Logically, perhaps, we should consider purposes first, but, as we have said, the concept is more difficult to handle than might be supposed, and there is much to be said for beginning with reading strategies, since they are relatively easy to grasp and knowledge of them bears fruit immediately for one's reading.

An example of a reading strategy is given in the *Purpose* section

The approach: an overview 7

above. We have identified it simply as a scanning strategy, which is satisfactory as a verbal label but does not go very far towards helping the reader to recognise it as behaviour in himself, to know when he is doing it and when he is not. In the next chapter we shall outline some techniques which will help him to do this and, of course, to recognise other reading strategies.

OUTCOME

By outcome we mean the result of our reading. Thus, if our reading purpose was to find the name of a particular author, possession of the name after reading would be a satisfactory outcome. Broadly, outcomes can be defined as the changes which take place in what we know, think and feel as a result of a particular piece of reading. It is as well to be precise about outcome. If we are vague about it then our reading tends to become ineffective and we are left making, perhaps, the dissatisfied comments upon ourselves of two of the people quoted above: 'I make different sense from an article if I read it again', and 'I can read all right, but I can't remember afterwards what I've just read'. (If he *had* been able to read 'all right' the outcome would have been less unsatisfactory.) It is, in the end, the outcome of our reading that provides the criterion of its effectiveness. For it to do that we must be able to measure outcome, or at least specify it precisely, and we must be honest about it.

REVIEW

By now it will have become apparent that the concepts we have been discussing are all related to each other. Purpose affects strategy; strategy affects outcome; and outcome, when related to purpose, provides the measure of the effectiveness of the strategy. Taken together they define the key features of reading to learn. If we want to improve our reading ability the things for us to concentrate on are clarifying our purposes, choosing the right strategies, and identifying precisely the outcomes of our reading. There is one thing more. In order to be sure that we have chosen the right strategy and carried it through successfully we have to check outcome against our original purpose. It is this operation that we have in mind when we talk about review.

Review extends more widely than simply checking outcome

8   *Reading to learn*

against purpose, for once we start on the operation we find that it involves us in a wholesale appraisal of all phases of the reading process. If outcome does not accord with purpose it could be that the purpose itself was wrongly formulated. Were we precise enough? Has our purpose changed as we have grown to know more about the subject? Or perhaps the purpose was correctly defined but the outcome imprecisely measured? Or possibly the relationship between outcome and purpose needs thinking about? Maybe the strategy was wrong anyway? All these, and a host of other questions, should come up during the review phase.

Even without going any further it can be seen that we have equipped ourselves with the beginnings of a vocabulary for conducting a conversation about the reading process. We are already able to refer some of the fragmentary remarks offered by people as descriptions of themselves as readers to one or other of the concepts we have introduced. 'I read word by word' and 'I read from the beginning to the end' are obviously strategies. While we cannot comment on their appropriateness until we know something about their relation to purposes, we probably do know that the person who replied 'I always read in the same way' is locked into a single strategy. 'I read the important bits usually' is a description of a strategy, too, and a much more sensible one. However, 'important' begs a lot of questions. It takes us at once to purpose. More subtly, it takes us to outcome. How do we know that what he thought was important was important? And so on with the other replies. We are beginning to be able to analyse our reading.

A model of reading to learn

What we have been doing is introducing a model of the whole process of reading to learn. The four concepts that we have just identified are the key components of the model. Separately, they identify parts of the reading process where we can intervene if we wish to develop our reading ability. Together they offer an opportunity for bringing the whole process of reading under more conscious control.

The process needs to be seen as a cyclical one. When you approach a reading task you clarify your purpose, choose an appropriate strategy, specify and assess the outcome of your reading, and then check back to see that your purpose is accomplished, i.e. review the whole operation. Review, however, may lead you to reassess your purpose. Purpose is never finally clarified until the final outcome is achieved and reviewed. Reclarification of purpose may lead to a different choice of strategy, and so on. Especially when you are a beginner *several* cycles of purpose-strategy-outcome-review (P-S-O-R) may be necessary. This may seem a formidable investment of time, and so it is. But it is an investment which in the long run will be repaid. It is better to go slowly at the beginning and build up the right habits than to skimp the basics and so never really know them. In time the process will become second nature, i.e. almost subconscious and quite speedy.

Purpose, strategy, outcome and review are the principal components of the model, but other things can be fitted into its framework too. It was suggested earlier that the prior knowledge and experience possessed by the advanced reader is an important advantage to him, and they should certainly be brought into the model. Similarly, features of the text, its structure, style and vocabulary, are important too, and must be taken into account. We shall see later how these and other things can be fitted into the model (and see also Fig. 1.1).

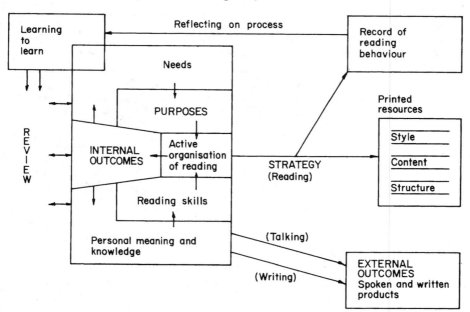

10 *Reading to learn*

P-S-O-R

What is important at this stage, however, is to be clear about purpose, strategy, outcome and review. Our first Activity is a very simple one but it may help the reader to confirm his understanding of the terms. At the same time it will, we hope, start the reader on the long process of self-evaluation with respect to reading.

Activity 1.1 **Developing an awareness of the reading to learn procedure**

Ask yourself:

Why are you reading this book? (Purpose)
How have you read this chapter so far? (Strategy)
What have you learnt? (Outcome)
Could you have approached the chapter differently? (Review)

Commentary

At this stage your answers will probably be rather general. You will probably have said something like 'I want to learn to read better' and 'I started at the beginning and read through'. No matter. As you proceed your answers will become more precise. Meanwhile, at least you are beginning to get an idea of what purpose, strategy, outcome and review are, and are starting to see how you can apply them to your reading.

Summary

The point that we hope we have made in this chapter is that people fail to become effective versatile readers for three basic reasons:

1 They are unable to formulate adequate operational purposes and therefore read in a rather vaguely orientated and non-specific way.

The approach: an overview 11

2 They are unaware of the ways in which they read. At best they have a crude idea of 'sometimes skimming', 'scanning', 'sometimes reading carefully', and 'sometimes going back and looking at something'. But many people are unable to control such strategies and believe that the process of reading is something that happens to them as they try to get at the meaning of the text, rather than being something which they can develop and use as a versatile learning skill.

3 They are unable to assess the quality of the learning outcome which is achieved during reading. Many readers, on putting down a book, can give only very vague and evasive answers to questions about exactly what they have learned.

Let us put this positively so that we know what we are aiming at: The effective reader is able to:

1 articulate a wide variety of realistic purposes;
2 choose from a wide variety of strategies in order to achieve specified purposes;
3 assess the quality of reading outcomes within the context of specified purposes;
4 review the whole process (purpose-strategy-outcome) in personal terms and systematically.

The hierarchical organisation of reading

There is one final general point to be made in this chapter before we move on to examining each of the principal components in turn. That is, reading is organised hierarchically. During reading one's awareness moves up and down through different levels or size of meaning unit. Sometimes one is concentrating on an individual word (when, say, unfamiliar letter clusters obtrude). At other times one can be skimming the words on a page in such a way that one isn't even aware of sentences or paragraphs. Sometimes, indeed, the relevant unit of meaning is the chapter. We can see these units as arranged in a hierarchy running from word to phrase to sentence to paragraph to section to chapter and so on (see Fig. 1.2).

The important thing for us to bear in mind is that the concepts we have introduced can also be arranged hierarchically. For example, we can think of purposes as arranged in a kind of

Figure 1.2 The hierarchical organisation of units of meaning

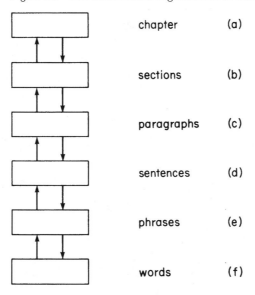

descending order. Our overall purpose in reading a chapter might be to find out about monetary policy (level (a) in Fig. 1.2). In particular we might want to know about how to define the supply of money, and we would formulate a purpose in those terms. This might correspond to a section in the chapter (level (b)) or to one or two paragraphs (level (c)). When we start reading the section we might be hung up over the meaning of a particular sentence. We would re-read the relevant part, adjusting our purpose to the more specific level (d) – 'to find out what the sentence means'. Or we might be puzzled by one particular word (e.g. 'bimetallism') and our concern would be to discover its meaning (level (f)).

If after reading we looked back over our purposes we would find it possible to arrange them in an ascending order, each level being part of the one above it. The same is true of strategies and outcomes.

2
Reading tactics and reading strategies

Overview

In this chapter we shall be concerned with reading strategies, the ways in which we read texts. Strategies are only part of good reading, as we saw in the last chapter, and it would be more logical to begin with reading purposes. However, beginning with strategies is easier, and also has the advantage of emphasising at once a key point: there is no one right way of reading. Different texts require different ways of reading – and the same text can be read differently if read with differing purposes. What we are trying to do is to increase your awareness of possible strategies and to help you to choose appropriately among them. Our particular aims in this chapter are: 1) to establish the existence of reading strategies; 2) to describe some of them; 3) to help you to begin to identify your own reading strategies. Once you are aware of them you may wish to change them. At any rate you will be in a better position to control them.

What are reading strategies?

But first, what are reading strategies? At the loosest level they are the ways we read. Suppose, for example, we pick up a book and read it straight through – that is one possible strategy. If we read, then make notes for a bit, read a bit more and so on, then that is another strategy. Strategies are not quite the same thing as tactics. Tactics are more local. If I come upon a passage which is difficult I might read it through to the end and try to get an overall sense of its meaning; or I might go carefully through, pondering each sentence and not moving on till I had got it fairly clear. These are two different tactics. Actually, I might well decide to use both – to first

14   *Reading to learn*

read the passage as a whole and then go back and take it again slowly. I might then finish by re-reading the passage as a whole. My overall reading strategy would then involve three separate reads. Each read would be tactically different.

We need, however, to be more precise. As we saw in the last chapter there are two major problems in improving our reading. The first is that the process itself is inaccessible to us. How do we read? Well, we don't really know. The second is that even when we do know we cannot easily describe it. We lack a language in which to talk about reading. The first thing we need, then, is a way of externalising what goes on when we read. We could do with some kind of reading record. The more precise the record can be, the more easily will we be able to find common terms with which to discuss it.

A means of obtaining such records was devised at the Centre for the Study of Human Learning at Brunel University, and it may be of interest to examine for a moment what the records showed. The records were obtained through the use of a reading recorder. With this machine the text is typed on a cylindrical roll of paper and can be viewed only through a narrow aperture which permits just two or three lines to be read at a time. The flow of the paper is controlled by a manually operated handle. Thus, if you want to read on you just keep turning the handle forward. If you want to refer back for anything you simply turn the handle in the reverse direction. It is easy to turn forward and back and after a few attempts you don't even notice that you are doing it. The handle is wired up to a pen which plots exactly what you have been doing on a piece of graph paper. The vertical axis of the graph shows position in the text. The horizontal axis shows progression in time. The record of someone reading a particular passage is shown in Fig. 2.1.

This record shows the reading of a four-hundred-line article in twenty minutes. We can see that the lines were not read at an even rate of $\frac{400}{20}$, i.e. twenty lines per minute. The first 100 lines were read in five minutes, i.e. at an average of 20 lines per minute, but then the reader spent five minutes not reading at all. In fact, he sat thinking for three minutes and made some notes, though this, of course, does not appear on the graph. From the tenth minute to the fifteenth he read more slowly from line 100 to line 150 ($\frac{150-100}{5} = \frac{50}{5} = 10$ lines per minute). Then he speeded up and read from lines 150 to 250 in two minutes. At line 250 he stopped

Figure 2.1 A simplified version of a record obtained on the reading recorder

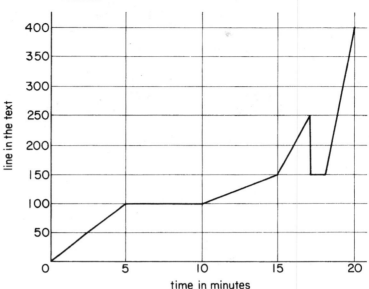

and turned quickly back to line 150. He stayed on line 150 for a minute. (Actually, he wasn't reading at this point, he was making notes). He then read very quickly and without stopping at all from line 150 to line 400 in two minutes (i.e. at a rate of $\frac{250}{2} = 125$ lines per minute).

A reading record like this immediately makes one wonder:

1 What was in the first 100 lines that made the reader pause and think after reading them?
2 He read lines 100 to 150 rather slowly. Why? What was it in lines 100 to 150 that was difficult to read?
3 Why did he go back from line 250 to line 150?
4 Why was it then so easy to read through from line 150 to the end?

If we explain that the first 100 lines were a simple introduction; the next 50 lines examined in detail the author's intentions; line 250 referred to an idea first dealt with in line 150; and the last 150 lines repeated the author's intentions more elaborately, then we can begin to infer quite a lot from the reader's behaviour.

16 *Reading to learn*

At any rate, from the record we can see something of the way in which the reader tackled the passage. What was inaccessible has become much more available. Moreover, it has been presented in a form which means that when we start discussing it at least we are talking about the same thing. Of course, the record does not tell us everything. We needed to supplement it by observations to know what the reader was doing when he wasn't reading. To really be sure we would need to discuss the record with the reader; but then, again, in our discussion with the reader we would have something concrete to go on, and we would find that the record jogged the reader's mind helpfully.

We are now in a position to be more precise about what we mean by a reading strategy and what we mean by reading tactics. When we are reading to learn we often read the text more than once. A complete reading record will consist of individual reads combined in various ways. Individual reads reveal the hesitations, the skips forward, the back-tracking etc. We can think of them as showing the person's reading tactics. The individual reads combine to reveal an overall reading strategy.

Kinds of reading tactics

We can begin, too, to characterise the reads, to put a name to the tactics. Research at the Centre for the Study of Human Learning shows that there are five basic types of read. On the reading recorder they appear as shown in Fig. 2.2.

a is a fairly rapid, more or less smooth, continuous read from beginning to end.

b is a slow read from beginning to end with detailed hesitations and possibly notes.

c is a read that shows continuous research backwards and forwards within the text.

d is a read usually associated with writing up one's notes and it shows the reader consulting a specific part of the text to check up on a particular point.

e is a fairly rapid read with few hesitations at selected parts of the text.

These basic read patterns combine .in various ways to form an overall reading strategy, and within the strategy one pattern can be

Reading tactics and reading strategies 17

Figure 2.2 Five basic patterns of reading

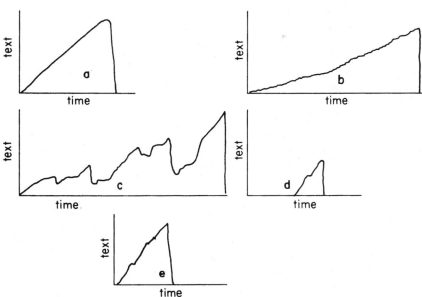

associated with different functions. Read **a**, the smooth read, for example, can be either the first read or the last read in a total reading strategy. If it appears as the first read then it may be performing an orientating or preparatory function. It shows the reader surveying the text with a view perhaps to thinking how he is going to tackle it. If the pattern appears at the end it is probably performing a checking function. The reader is reviewing the text to make sure that he has got it right, that he has missed nothing. In that case one sometimes finds the record showing a few hesitations or some back-tracking, indicating that attention is being given to particular parts of the text. The pattern then becomes similar to that of type **c**.

Although the smooth read can play an important part in an overall reading strategy, it is not in itself associated with much learning going on. The smoothness of the read indicates that there is little engagement with particular parts of the text. This could be for two reasons. Firstly, it might be because the reader is already familiar with the text. Alternatively, it might be because the reader

18 *Reading to learn*

never gets 'into' the text. In the first case, if the reader is tested afterwards he may show quite a lot of knowledge of the text. In the second case he might show very little. What this points to is that in itself the read record is never sufficient to tell us all that is going on. We need to supplement the record by discussion with the reader (ourself, if we are the reader) and by comparison with the outcome of our read – by testing whether we have in fact obtained all we wanted to from the passage.

Read **b**, the item read, shows a reader plodding steadily through the text, looking neither to left nor to right of him, as it were, but carefully reading every part of the text as it comes up. There is very little skipping or back-tracking. Every part of the passage is given equal attention, no matter whether it is dense theory or inessential diversion. The passage is processed item by item. The items may be small units of meaning such as phrases or sentences, or they may represent larger units of meaning such as groups of sentences or paragraphs. The reader dwells on each in turn, as is indicated by the hesitations shown in the reading record.

This type of read shows a reading tactic which is particularly useful for tackling a passage containing many facts which the reader is seeking to identify and memorise. Item reads are always associated with good scores in multiple-choice tests and any tests demanding factual knowledge or recall at the literal level. Where, however, the passage is not of that sort and the reader's purpose is not to acquire factual information – where, for example, he wants to understand an argument or a theory – the tactic is less useful. Unfortunately, this type of read shows exactly the way in which many less efficient readers tackle a text. They labour through it bit by bit, no matter the nature of the passage nor their purpose in reading it. Not only that – they read all passages in the same way. This is a very inflexible and inefficient approach to reading, and one of the first things which anyone who wants to improve their reading has to do is to discard it. An item read may be a perfectly sensible tactic to employ as part of a particular reading strategy: when, for example, part of a text being read contains much detailed factual information which it is necessary to acquire in order to appreciate an argument being developed in another section of the passage. If it is the only tactic which a reader employs, however, then the reader has problems. But, broadly, one can say that the more selective the purpose in terms of the content of the text, the fewer the hesitations in the read. A really efficient reader shows hesitations only in those parts of the text relevant to his or her chosen purpose.

Read **c**, the search read, shows the reader skipping positively backwards and forwards in an attempt to trace the author's meaning. 'Signposts' in the text (which we will discuss later, but of which this remark is itself an example) refer the reader back to ideas discussed previously or forward to ideas yet to be encountered, and help him make connections between them. With this read the reader is trying to construct relationships. This tactic can be particularly useful when the reader is trying to get to grips with a complex argument.

Read **d**, as was said earlier, is not really a true complete read. It is a part read, showing the consultation of the text for a specific point. It is the kind of quick check with the text that someone might make when they were writing up their notes into an essay. It is also, it may be said, the kind of read that you sometimes get when the reader is not really bothering at all!

Read **e** we have also referred to earlier. It is basically a smooth read with one or two marked hesitations showing where attention is being given to particular parts of the text. This pattern is usually explicable either in terms of the structure or content of the passage being read or in terms of a particular purpose on the part of the reader.

These five basic patterns of reading are in a sense 'ideal' types: in practice, reads tend to be less pure, not always clearly identifiable as one type. In any case they only give us a guide as to what is going on. In the end only the reader really knows what was passing through his mind when he was reading, and even he often finds it very hard to remember precisely. What the reading record can do is to jog the reader's mind. Taken together with the text it can permit specific points in the reading process to be identified and discussed. And overall it gives a pretty good clue to the particular tactics the reader has been employing.

Tactics and strategies

The complete record of the way in which a reader engages with a particular reading task may include several individual reads of the sort we have been discussing. Individual reads can be thought of as showing the reader's tactics with respect to a passage – and they combine to display the overall strategy employed for the reading task as a whole. Choice of strategy will depend on the reader's purpose, the nature of the passage, and the reader's own personality. There is no one right strategy. Different strategies suit different occasions. However, we can offer some general guidance. Figure 2.3 below illustrates a reading strategy found to be especially effective for answering multiple-choice questions.

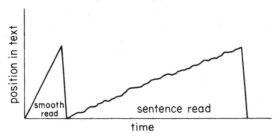

Figure 2.3 A reading strategy found to be effective for answering multiple-choice questions

The complete record shows that two individual reads were employed, a smooth read and an item read. A smooth read was used by the reader to alert himself to the general lay-out of the article. This was followed by a detailed item read (in this case the size of the item was the sentence).

The record is in fact that of a particular reader. In a test afterwards he performed well on multiple-choice questions, which tended to require literal recall, but he was much less successful in writing a summary. What he produced was a rather arbitrary selection of facts which lacked any real sense of the overall argument and implications of the passage.

Figure 2.4 shows the record of a successful summary writer. The record shows that the smooth read and the item read were also employed by this reader. In addition, however, he also used a paragraph read, a search read and a final smooth read. We have found that the paragraph read (which is a kind of item read) tends to be associated with the organisation of the reader's understanding into larger units. The search read accompanies the process of really getting to grips with the complex flow of meaning. And the final

Figure 2.4 A reading strategy found to be effective for summarising a difficult text

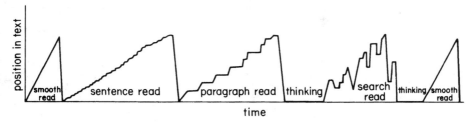

smooth read shows the reader checking and confirming his already formulated understandings. The first smooth read is useful for getting a general idea of what the passage is all about, and so guiding the reader in his subsequent choice of tactics, but in itself it would not result in high scores either on multiple-choice tests or on essay questions. Incidentally, we have found that summary writers who make use of the strategy shown in Fig. 2.4 are usually also successful on multiple-choice tests. What is more, they retain their knowledge longer than people who just use the strategy shown in Fig. 2.3.

We shall say more about strategies in later chapters. Our purpose so far in this chapter has been to establish the existence of tactics and strategies in reading to learn and to give a preliminary indication of what we mean by them. What we want to do now is to help you to begin to identify your own reading tactics and strategies.

Activity 2.1   Tracking your own reading

Our first activity is intended to make you more aware, at a fairly loose level, of the way in which you read. We shall ask you to track the way you read a particular passage. To do that you will need to make use of the necessary conventions shown in Fig. 2.5, *so would you familiarise yourself with the symbols* before beginning.

We shall now describe the technique for using the symbols. Take a pencil in your hand and as you read trace in the margin your progression through the text. Try to be aware of the movement of your eyes from one line to the next. If you pause or make notes indicate this by putting ⪋ for pause and N for notes. If you search backwards trace the pencil to the line you re-read and mark with an arrow ↑. If you skip forward draw a dotted line ⋮ and mark with an arrow ↓ the line you select to read.

Almost certainly you will find this difficult the first time you do it, and it may well disturb the habitual pattern of your reading. Do not worry. Most people find that after a few goes they can manage quite well. However, it is a good idea to *practise the technique* on a few

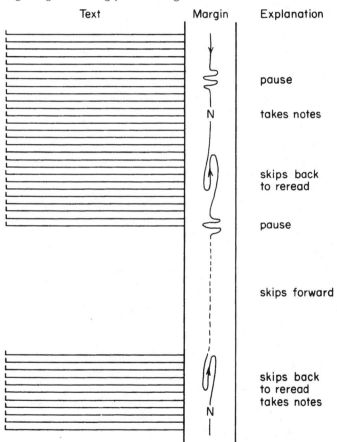

Figure 2.5 Tracking your reading

Reading tactics and reading strategies 23

passages before coming to the one you have chosen for the exercise.

When you think you can use the technique without too much strain, *choose a passage*. It should be at least 700 words long and taken preferably from an article or book that you are studying. A section from a textbook would be fine. Ask yourself what it is that you hope to learn from the passage. As you read, bear in mind that purpose. Do not read slackly. Read it genuinely to learn something.

Now *read the passage*, tracking yourself in the margin. You may need to read it more than once. To avoid confusing the two reading records you could use the opposite margin for tracking the second reading. If you need to read it a third or more times use an extra slip of paper as a temporary margin.

You now have a rudimentary reading record. Use it to *talk yourself back through the read* you have just made, trying to remember exactly what it was you did and why you did it. Start at the beginning of your pencil track and move slowly along it with your finger. Try to remember, with the aid of the markings and by referring to the text, what you were doing at particular points. Your talk-back might go like this:

I read the text twice. On the first occasion I wanted to get a good preview, so that next time round I could select important bits. On the second 'read' I zoned in on these bits, and searched between paragraphs for . . . . I paused on lines so and so because:

    I couldn't understand the phrase/term/word
    I found it interesting
    It was important for my purpose
    I disagreed with the author
    I made notes
    I was daydreaming
    I was linking it to what went before
    etc.
I skipped forward on lines so and so because:
    I could tell it wasn't relevant
    I knew about it already
    I was challenged by the author
    etc.
I made notes on lines so and so because:
    I wanted to recall this exactly

24 *Reading to learn*

> I wanted to check it later
> I thought I could use these for reconsidering my outcome
> It's a habit I've got – always make notes
>
> My notes were:
>> Very detailed
>> Very brief
>> Actually maps
>> Actually lists
>> etc.
>
> In my second read, I searched back and forward:
>> between sentences in para. so-and-so
>> because I . . . .
>> between paragraphs so-and-so and so-and-so
>> because I . . . .
>> between phrases in sentence so-and-so
>> because I . . . .

You may find it helpful to make notes. An example is given in the Appendix at the end of the chapter (Rhianon's read).

When you have finished stand back from the details and ask yourself some questions about the read as a whole.

How long did you take?
Did you read it more than once?
Was the way you read it different when you read it again?
How was it different?
Did you read smoothly?
Did you skip forward or track back?
Did you pause in the right places?
Did you make notes in the right places?

and then, of course, the hard question:

If you had to read it again, what changes would you make in the way you read it?

At this stage you probably will not be able to say very much on this, for you lack terms in which to discuss the way you read. We shall be giving you some of those terms in later chapters. Already, however, you should be becoming a little more aware of what goes on when

Reading tactics and reading strategies 25

you read. The record you made of your read, rudimentary though it was, should have helped to jog your memory and helped you to recall some of the particular things you did, particular hesitations, doubts, ideas, particular moves in your own individual reading game. More than this the activity will not achieve. It is just a first step towards increasing your awareness.

Repeat the exercise a few times. You will find yourself becoming gradually more and more aware of yourself reading. After a while you will not need to keep a pencil track in the margin. The tracking will be in your mind.

If you are doing this activity in a group you may find it interesting to compare your read with someone else's. The pencil tracking in the margin will reveal similarities and dissimilarities of approach. In itself that is not very significant, but in describing your route through the passage to each other you will find first of all that you will become clearer in your mind about how exactly you read the passage and secondly that alternative ways of reading the passage, alternative tactics, are thrown up.

Another task you may like to do is to look at a reading record of someone reading a different passage. In Appendix 3 to this chapter we give an extract from such a record. Not only is the text different but the reader's purpose is probably different, too. She wanted to evaluate the findings of a report that reading standards have declined in recent years in Britain. The reader is, in fact, a teacher in a junior school and her concerns, knowledge of the topic, and background values are also probably different from your own. Nevertheless, you may find it interesting to see how she tackled the passage. Some of her comments on herself – those on purpose, for instance – will make more sense when you have read a little further. She has a great familiarity with terms for talking about reading than you have at this stage. Yet you should gain some idea of the critical conversation you can have with yourself about reading.

Activity 2.1 is a sensitisation exercise. It is designed to make you more sensitive to the way you read. It works, however, in a general, rather loose, way. If you are to work on your reading tactics and strategies and so improve them you will need to be able to think of them in more precise terms. Activity 2.2 is designed to help you do that.

Earlier in the chapter we showed how by using a reading recorder it is possible to depict graphically the way someone reads a

26 *Reading to learn*

passage and to identify certain basic patterns, certain reading tactics, which combine to form reading strategies. We want now to help you to describe your own reading in ways which will enable you to relate it to the basic patterns we have identified.

This is one activity where you will definitely need the help of an observer, so if you are not doing this as part of a group you will have to enlist someone else beforehand. The observer will take the place of the reading recorder. The reading records produced in this way will not be quite as informative as those produced by the machine but they will make it fairly easy to compare your reads with the basic types described earlier.

For this activity you will also need a cardboard viewing window and some squared paper. The window is very simple and takes about two minutes to make. Directions are given in the Appendix at the end of the chapter.

Activity 2.2   Recording your reading tactics

Prepare a cardboard viewing window. This allows you to see 3 to 4   1
lines of text at a time. Number the lines in your chosen text on the   2
right hand side, as illustrated on this page. To begin with choose a   3
short text consisting of one or two pages only. *As an initial practice, use*   4
this page. Get hold of an observer and check that both of you   5
understand how to use the recording sheet in Appendix II. This is   6
divided into two parts. The raw data table (a) is used to record the   7
sequence in which the lines are read. As the reader moves the viewing   8
window upwards and downwards the number associated with each   9
line is revealed. The observer notes these down on the sheet under   10
the heading *Line.* The *Order* represents all the number of lines in the   11
text in sequence. These are entered in beforehand in the margin.   12
Draw up some raw data tables and read the page again, using the   13
window and recording the process. Your observer need not write   14
down every line number but he or she should concentrate on   15
repeating the number on the record if you hesitate, and should note   16
the line numbers if you backtrack or skip forward. When the   17
observations are complete you can summarise them in the form of a   18
read record (b). The observations in the raw data table are plotted   19
one by one onto graph paper. Divide ordinary paper into squares if   20

Reading tactics and reading strategies 27

you do not have any. It is also useful to record how long you took to 21
read the text, by noting the time at the beginning and the end. 22

When you and your observer have practised this two or three 23
times, choose a passage in the way you did for Activity 2.1, remind 24
yourself of what it is you are looking for in the text (information, 25
theory), and read the text genuinely seeking to learn from it. You 26
may need to read it more than once. Record each read and plot it in 27
the way described above. 28

Afterwards, prepare a reading record for your whole read in the 29
way illustrated in Figs. 2.3 and 2.4. This will show you your reading 30
strategy. 31

Now talk yourself back through the read in the way that you did 32
in Activity 2.1. You will need to relate your record to the text, 33
which you can do by referring to the line numbers. Remember to 34
stand back at the end and review the read as a whole. Could you 35
have approached the passage differently? Could you have distri- 36
buted your time differently, spending more time on some parts of 37
the text, less on others? 38

Your awareness of your own reading will still be tentative at this
stage. However, this activity should produce 'harder' data for you
to take into account, so that you should be able to be more precise
about the way you tackled the passage. You may even be able to
identify patterns in your read which correspond to the basic
patterns ('tactics') which we described earlier in the chapter.

You may find it easier to do this if you repeat the activity in a
slightly different way. If you can get your partner to time you as you
read you will get information in the same form as you would
through using the reading recorder. The observer should record
your position in the text (by ticking the line number) at regular
intervals. Ten-second intervals are best if he or she can manage it.
Draw up your graph with time on the horizontal scale. That will
give you graphs comparable with those we took from the reading
recorder. You may now be able to identify more precisely the
particular reading tactics you have employed.

Do not worry if the patterns are not quite as clear as those shown
in our 'typical' graphs. They will become more so. As you become
more skilled in monitoring your own reading you will be able to

28 *Reading to learn*

differentiate your reads more clearly. Your smooth read will become smoother, your item read more like the basic pattern. Our aim at the moment is to help you to begin to know when you are using a particular kind of reading tactic. With practice you will be able to choose your tactic consciously. Control over your reading will grow.

What you should be aiming for is to dispense with your observer altogether. He will be helpful in the early stages because he provides firmer, more objective data – better feedback – but your aim should be to do without him. You should be able to rely on your own introspective sense of how you are reading. Practise with an observer a few times, but practise with a view to being able to tell for yourself what reading tactic you are employing.

When you first do this activity it will take you some time, possibly an hour. You need to prepare the materials, read the passage, translate the data into the form of a reading record, and then talk yourself back through your read. After you have done it two or three times the operations will become more automatic and the whole process will be completed far more speedily. At that point it is a good idea to use the activity as a warming-up exercise while you are concentrating on the suggestions put forward in later chapters.

Summary

This chapter has introduced the concept of 'reading behaviour'. You have been shown how to record your reading of a text so that you can identify the ways in which you read. Becoming more aware of your own reading behaviour may encourage you to experiment with different ways of reading. The activities have demonstrated that different kinds of tactics and strategies can be employed as a person reads. The idea of a process conversation was introduced in Chapter 1. 'Reading strategy' represents one basic term which is important to understand when one converses about effective ways of reading to learn.

Reading tactics and reading strategies 29

Appendix 2.1 Viewing window

Using the dimensions shown below, mark out a window in the centre of a piece of thin card about 100 mm × 20 mm. Cut this out. You should be able to see three lines of text through the window.

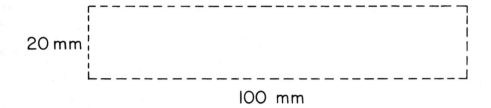

30   *Reading to learn*

Appendix 2.2 Recording sheet for use in Activity 2.2

(a) Raw data table

Order	Line	Order	Line
1	1	35	31
2	2	36	32
3	3	37	33
4	4	38	34
5	5	39	35
6	6	40	32
7	7	41	31
8	8	42	30
9	9 ⎫	43	29
10	9 ⎬ H	44	27
11	9 ⎭	45	26
12	10	46	27
13	11	47	28
14	12	48	29
15	13	49	30
16	14	50	31
17	15	51	31 ⎫
18	16	52	31 ⎬ H
19	17	53	31 ⎭
20	18	54	32 ⎫ H
21	19 ⎫	55	32 ⎭
22	19 ⎬ H	56	33
23	19 ⎭	57	34
24	20	58	35
25	21	59	36
26	22	60	37
27	23	61	38
28	24	62	39
29	25	63	40
30	26	64	41
31	27	65	42
32	28	66	43
33	29	67	44
34	30		

H = hesitation

Reading tactics and reading strategies 31

Appendix 2.2 Recording sheet for use in Activity 2.2—*continued*

(b) Read record

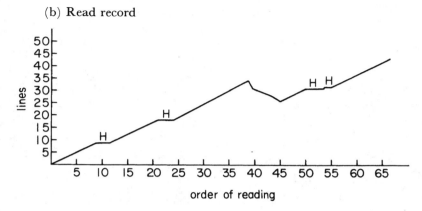

Note. The vertical axis shows the *number* of the line and the horizontal axis shows the sequential *order* in which the lines were read.

32 *Reading to learn*

Appendix 2.3 Rhianon's read record

Text	Margin	Explanation
of functional literacy, ability is used. 1) of five and one-half of age, four million— 24 per cent of the popula- that in a population of consequently, need to be 5 per cent of the entire rate is estimated to of United Nations; population is unable to population is almost en- shocking, as many as ranging from 10 per fifteen and above with a very disquieting rather than being on the to thirty million to the circumstance that not been enough to keep **our world of today** has not been given the proper way, cannot live of a fundamental access to one of the most said: 'Learning is 'living the ability to read is an living in every corner of conference spoke on this ability, half of the the human rights. They and technology give us to also be excluded from the written documents.'	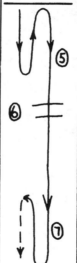	④ The complexity of the written list I thought was irrelevant to my purposes. I skipped all reading, until numbers stopped. ⑤ Trying to look at paragraph as a unit, and deciding what important idea it could give. But to no avail, re-read, picking out the different locations of key words. ⑥ Re-read my purposes, refresh my memory because I usually get clogged up in irrelevant detail – habit I have ⑦ With purpose in mind, read paragraph, skipped back, as sentence defined my aim. ⑧ Remembered – quotation not significant with previous reading of text. ⑨ Thought position key sentence may be first sentence, but nothing concerning details evident.

Reading tactics and reading strategies 33

Appendix 2.3 Rhianon's read record—*continued*

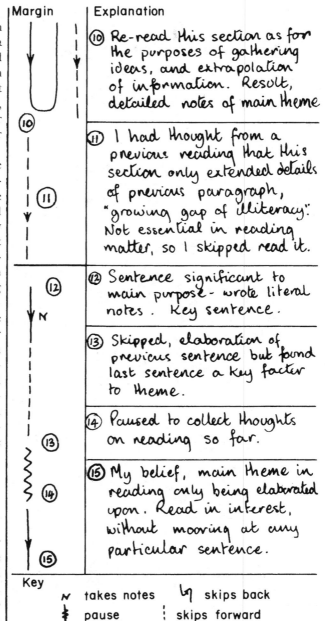

Text	Margin	Explanation
its traditional pattern for the fulfillment of a of transportation and all corners of this earth of technical development and, therefore, There will be fewer in any part of our		⑩ Re-read this section as for the purposes of gathering ideas, and extrapolation of information. Result, detailed notes of main theme
governing countries were was created. Demo- where the citizens are strong political demand gap between low is to a great extent acquired national inde-		⑪ I had thought from a previous reading that this section only extended details of previous paragraph, "growing gap of illiteracy". Not essential in reading matter, so I skipped read it.
percentage—and the high actual and ever-growing disease in the world, we serious handicap for that we know. In		⑫ Sentence significant to main purpose - wrote literal notes. Key sentence.
as the most irrecon- everywhere in the world understanding and co- but most stubborn nations within them- the literates and the		⑬ Skipped, elaboration of previous sentence but found last sentence a key factor to theme.
		⑭ Paused to collect thoughts on reading so far.
must realise that their the properties of the by U Thant, General session of the United in Geneva. He also gap between the rich		⑮ My belief, main theme in reading only being elaborated upon. Read in interest, without moving at any particular sentence.

Key
∼ takes notes ↰ skips back
⇟ pause ⋮ skips forward

3
Reading purposes

Overview

In this chapter we shall be discussing reading purposes. As we shall see, being clear about what our purposes are in reading a particular text is really quite important in reading to learn. The trouble is that we are often nowhere near clear enough. Just as, we suggested in the last chapter, people are often very vague about the way they actually read, so they are vague about their purposes in reading. What we shall try to do in this chapter is to help you to become much more precise about your reading purposes. We want you to be able to distinguish more sharply between them. When you can do that you will be able to relate your tactics and strategies in reading more appropriately to your purposes. And when you can do *that* you will find that you have tightened up the whole way in which you read to learn and can perform the whole process more successfully.

The nature of reading purposes

Purpose is important in reading to learn for two reasons. Firstly, the way you read a text varies with your purpose. If you are reading it because you are going to be examined on it you will read it in a very different way from the way you would if you were reading it for fun. Or if you are reading it to seek out one item of information you will read it in a different way from the way you would if you were seeking out several items or trying to understand a complex theory. If you were trying to identify one item you would probably skim through the passage and 'not really read the passage at all' (though

Reading purposes 35

in fact you *would* be reading it; it is just that you would be employing a special kind of reading tactic). If you were trying to absorb a difficult theory skimming would not do.

Secondly, in order to check whether you have read a passage successfully you have to check against something, and that can only be your purpose in reading. If after reading the passage you can remember only one item, say a particular date, that's fine if your purpose was to find that particular item but not much good if your purpose was to understand the general theoretical argument. We shall argue later that an essential part of improving your ability to read to learn is checking how well the particular tactics you have employed have worked. That must be done by reference to purpose.

Being clear about one's purposes in reading is, then, important. But what do we mean by being clear about reading purposes? If someone asks us what our purpose is in reading a particular passage or book we can usually make some sort of reply: 'I am trying to get clear what is meant by M3', or 'I am trying to get clear about monetarism because I've got to write an essay on it'. This is fine so far as it goes, but we really need to go further if we are to improve our reading effectiveness. We need to be more precise about the *kind* of purpose involved. In the case of M3, for example, is our purpose to acquire factual information or are we trying to grasp a concept? As we saw in the last chapter, it will make a difference to our choice of tactic which of these it is. Roughly, if we are looking for facts we might use an item read, whereas if we are trying to understand a concept a search read might be better. What we have to do, then, is learn how to classify our purposes, to be able to say that this particular purpose is to do with the acquisition of factual information whereas that particular purpose is to do with the acquisition of concepts.

Before we do that, however, it is worth taking just a little time to think more generally about reading purposes.

Suppose you were asked to undertake a learning assignment which required you to consult a number of books: a project, say. How would you go about organising your reading for it? You would probably say 'I need to know about this and that, so I'd better get books on those topics.' If, say, your subject were 'Monetary policy and the British economy 1977–81' you might say, 'I need to know something general about the banking system so I'd

36 *Reading to learn*

better get that book: then I'd better get a book on the economic background of the period, but then there's this monetarism business; I'd better get hold of Friedman's articles: and what about a critique of them?' and so on. The books would probably be dauntingly fat and when you were faced with them you would probably say 'I can't read all that lot. What is it I really need to know?' And so you would start to narrow down your reading purposes and make them more specific.

Now there are some points to be made about this process. The first is that reading purposes can be arranged in levels of generality to form a kind of hierarchy. Thus 'to find out something about the banking system' is at a high level of generality, whereas 'to find out what a bank deposit is' is at a much lower level of generality. If we have four or five statements of this sort, each representing a reading purpose, we could arrange them in ascending order of generality to form a purpose hierarchy.

The second point is that arranging purposes in this way provides useful guidance in organising our reading. If we think the matter through beforehand, for example, we may realise that to achieve one particular purpose we may need to read a whole book, whereas to achieve other purposes we may need only to consult specific chapters or parts of chapters.

The point is obvious; but our experience is that year after year students enter higher education without having apparently grasped it. Their reading for assignments is badly organised and inefficient. They spend a lot of time reading (not infrequently, too much time) but because their reading is not specific enough their efforts are often wasted. Improvement begins with the clarification of reading purpose. That is the way to specificity.

Note that clarification is important at all levels in the hierarchy. Clarification at the higher levels can help the reader to identify appropriate resources – books, articles, tapes, etc. – and guide him in the way he uses them. Clarification at lower levels guides the reader in his choice of tactics to tackling a particular section or paragraph.

Note, too, that purpose-clarification is not a once and for all job which you do just at the beginning of a reading task. Clarification at the beginning is certainly important – it can have a considerable impact on the overall efficiency with which the task is carried out. But when you start reading in a new area you often don't know the

Reading purposes 37

ground well enough to be able to say in advance what aspects of the subject you will need to go into. Your thinking about purposes at the start will inevitably be provisional and will need updating as you read more extensively.

Activity 3.1   Constructing a purpose hierarchy

This activity is intended to begin the process of raising your level of awareness of reading purposes. Choose some learning task which you have been assigned and which requires quite a lot of reading. It would help if you had some knowledge of the subject before you started. Ask yourself what you need to do in order to be able to perform the task ('I need to find out about X, Y, etc.'). Then, with respect to each of your answers, ask yourself what you need to do to achieve *them*; and so on. Suppose, for example, your topic were the one mentioned earlier, 'Monetary policy and the British economy 1977–81'. If you asked yourself what you needed to know in order to write on that subject you might well come up with several answers of the sort 'I need to know something about the banking system', 'I must find out about the economic background of the period', and so on. But then for each of these answers sub-questions can be put. *What* do I need to know about the banking system? (I might need to know about how banks create credit, for example, but have absolutely no need to know about the internal organisational structure of banks.) Similarly, with respect to the economic background I might need to know about the general level of activity, the movement of prices, and the balance of payments but *not* about the fortunes of the steel industry, sales of motor cars, or whatever. Naturally you won't be able to supply all the answers at once, especially if the field is relatively unfamiliar, but almost certainly you will be able to supply some, and fill in others as you go. (Incidentally, this is a good revision exercise for a topic with which you are familiar; it helps you to become clear about the relationships between different parts of the field.)

When you have done this part of the activity you should have before you a number of reading tasks each of which is in fact the expression of a particular reading purpose. Now arrange those items in the form of a purpose hierarchy. Put the most general ones

38 *Reading to learn*

('to find out about the banking system') at the top and the more specific ones lower down. You will find, of course, that your hierarchy takes the form of an inverted tree, with one general purpose at the top, dividing into two or three main purpose-branches, each of which divides into several more and so on.

The point of Activity 3.1 is to start you thinking more sharply about your reading purposes. However, exhibiting the relationships between purposes in the form of a hierarchy has other incidental advantages. It displays, for example, the pattern of reading with respect to a particular assignment. Purposes can be related very precisely to resources.

One way of showing this relationship, if you are systematically minded, is through a purpose-resource grid. It is very easy to draw one up. You list reading purposes down the left hand side of your paper, put resources (books, articles, etc.) across the top of your paper, and where a particular reading purpose can be met by reference to a particular text or resource you put a tick. A resource which caters for a wide variety of purposes will have a lot of ticks in its column, and, conversely, a purpose which requires you to consult a wide range of resources will have a long row of ticks alongside it. From the reader's point of view this enables you to see at a glance which sources are most significant and in which connection. The grid may well be of most use, however, to teachers setting assignments, for it indicates the nature of the demand for particular resources and helps them to plan ahead in terms of availability.

At lower levels in the purpose hierarchy readers will be defining their purpose in reading particular texts: reading Passage A, for example, to find out details of how to do an experiment, reading Text B, perhaps, to identify images of death and desolation, or reading Chapter C to select examples of a particular concept. Purpose clarification at this level of detail will not, of course, be done when you first start thinking about the assignment. The need for it will arise as you go along. It is important, however, that you *should* do it as you go along. Time spent on talking to yourself through your reading purpose is time well spent if you are hoping to improve your reading ability: and you should get into the habit of

Reading purposes   39

briefly reviewing your purposes before you tackle *any* significant reading to learn assignment.

Specifying purposes in terms of comprehension

Once the specific questions which represent the bottom level of the purpose hierarchy have been identified, it is useful to consider them in relation to what has to be done to the relevant items in the text to achieve a satisfactory outcome. Different purposes may require different kinds of comprehension; and different kinds of comprehension may imply different reading tactics and strategies.

Activity 3.2   **Reading purposes and comprehension**

Consider the following specific purposes taken from the lower level of students' purpose hierarchies and try to classify them in terms of the kind of comprehension skills involved. 'To find the names of characters', for example, involves identification skills and not much more; 'to find the name of the chief character' involves identification plus judgement – out of several characters which is the chief one?

1 To locate statistical figures
2 To find a description of an event
3 To check a method for preparing a product
4 To find the details of an experiment
5 To identify examples of a concept
6 To select and identify main points and summarise them
7 To abstract the main theme
8 To evaluate the style of a passage
9 To identify the structure of the author's argument
10 To evaluate the author's point of view on a theoretical issue
11 To evaluate the significance of particular imagery
12 To infer details not stated by the author

This can be a discussion exercise if you are doing it as a member of a group, but even if you approach the activity this way it is as well to begin by thinking the items through for yourself. Purposes 1 to 5

40 *Reading to learn*

involve scanning the text for literal answers. Once the relevant part of the test has been identified little more has to be done. Selection and identification of the correct answers are the comprehension skills demanded. Purposes 6 and 7 demand selection and identification skills. Bits of the text have to be assessed for relevance and judgement has to be made based on the reader's knowledge and on the content of the text as a whole. The relevant items have to be *reorganised* and *synthesised* into a coherent structure which summarises or abstracts the original text. Purposes 8–12? Well, they, too, require the selection and identification of relevant items, followed by judgement, reorganisation and synthesis.

Purposes 6–12 demand quite complex skills on the part of the reader. Relevant parts of the text have to be temporarily held in the memory while other parts are sampled. It seems likely that a different reading strategy will be needed from that required for purposes 1–5. A continuous search backwards and forwards may be necessary to relate and organise the relevant items into a coherent whole.

Kinds of purpose and kinds of comprehension

Activity 3.2 started us thinking about the relationship between reading purposes and comprehension skills. What we need now is a rather more systematic way of describing the relationship so that we can be more precise in our identification of particular comprehension skills. Various people have tried to provide a systematic classification of the comprehension skills which relate to different purposes for reading. The two best known of these are the classification systems of Bloom and Barrett (Bloom, 1956; Barrett, 1968). Both describe their systems as 'taxonomies'. A taxonomical classification is one so constructed that lower-order categories are subsumed by higher-order ones. The concept has its roots in biological practice, where, for example, living things are classified into animals and plants, animals into vertebrates and invertebrates, vertebrates into fishes, amphibia, reptiles, birds and mammals, and so on, and is well suited to represent the ways in which reading purposes and levels of comprehension relate one to another.

Table 3.1 presents a purpose taxonomy (derived from Bloom and Barrett but more suitable to our requirements) which can help the

Reading purposes 41

reader in determining the kind of mental operations, the particular comprehension skills, which he needs to use with respect to the text.

Table 3.1   A purpose taxonomy: A classification of comprehension skills

5	*Extrapolation*	Inferences beyond the text. Implications in other situations. Creative divergence from author's ideas. Use of imagination. Putting forward a hypothesis.
4	*Evaluation*	Appraisal of opinion, arguments. Critique of style. Judgements of main theme, details. Assessment of message's importance value.
3	*Appreciation*	Appreciation of style, mood, nuances. Structure of text, choice of words. Metaphors, analogies, similes. Quality of rhetoric, images. Range and nature of argument. Aesthetic response.
2	*Reorganisation, analysis and synthesis*	Identification of ideas and their restructuring into summary or abstract. Classification of ideas. Paraphrase. Interpretation of viewpoint.
1	*Literal*	Identification and remembering of details, ideas, facts, opinions, concepts, instructions, examples, inferences, criticisms, 'signposts'.

Activity 3.3   Using the purpose taxonomy to classify comprehension skills

Read the text 'The mystery of the chemical cabinet' and the questions which follow. The questions express particular reading purposes. Classify the questions with reference to the purpose taxonomy and to the text.

From the question alone you will get a good idea of what your answer should be. Questions act as advanced organisers of your reading: they direct your attention to certain kinds of item, certain kinds of skill. For this reason it is often a good idea to think of reading purposes in terms of questions. However, you will probably need, at this stage, to consult the text to see what kind of detail, what kind of operation, is necessary to answer the question.

42 *Reading to learn*

As, in clarifying each question, you locate the relevant parts of the text, underline them in different colours for each question. At the end of the exercise look back at the pattern of colour arrived at. It will show you how purpose influences the relevance of different parts of the text. You will see that different purposes concentrate your attention on different parts of the text. Choice of reading tactics and reading strategies will need to take this into account.

The mystery of the chemical cabinet

Today, developing a photograph is quite simple. You just dip the exposed film into the right chemical solution and out comes the negative. Then you expose the negative to the right type of light and you have a photo – or two, or three, or as many as you want.

A little more than a hundred years ago, however, developing a photograph was quite a different matter. Men had not yet learned how to make negatives. A plate, on which the image was exposed, was developed and then it was made into the photo; no copies could be made.

But crude as they were, these first photos were better than none at all; and until a man named Louis Daguerre discovered the above method for developing them, there were no photos . . .

One morning in 1837 Louis Daguerre went to his workshop. His friend, Joseph Niepce, had left an exposed plate with him the night before. He had put it in a chemical cabinet.

Daguerre was trying to find a way to develop photographic images, so faint they could hardly be seen. And those pictures were the reverse in light and shade of the picture that was taken. In other words, what had been black was white and what had been white was black. They were like negatives, not positives.

Daguerre went to the cabinet and took out the plate. When he saw it, he nearly dropped it! The page was developed! And the lights and shades were the same as those of the image photographed! This was a positive. What could have developed it?

In great excitement, Daguerre looked inside the cabinet. As always, there were a lot of bottles and jars of chemicals. He checked them all over. There was nothing new.

Then he studied the cabinet thoughtfully. One of those chemicals must be the developing agent. But which one was it?

Reading purposes 43

That night Daguerre took just one chemical bottle from the cabinet. He put in another exposed plate. The next morning he hurried to his workshop and opened the cabinet. Eagerly he took out the plate. It, too, was developed. The chemical he had taken out, then, was not the developing agent.

That night, Daguerre put a fresh plate in the cabinet. At the same time he took out another bottle. In the morning this plate was developed too.

Night after night Daguerre put another plate in the cabinet. Night after night he took out another bottle. And each day it was the same story. The plate was always developed.

At last there was just one more bottle in the cabinet. 'Surely this last jar contains the developing agent I'm looking for', said Daguerre to his friend Niepce. As he spoke he put in a fresh plate with the last bottle left in the cupboard. 'If I'm right, this plate will be developed in the morning.'

And sure enough, in the morning the plate was developed. Daguerre was jubilant. He was sure he had found the right chemical.

He lost no time in trying it out on another plate. But he was sorely disappointed and greatly puzzled. The chemical did not work! It had no effect on the exposed plate!

'Then how', asked Niepce, 'did the plate you put in the cabinet last night become developed if this chemical will not work? There was no other bottle in the cupboard. It MUST have been this one.'

'Well', said Daguerre, 'I am going to put another plate in the empty cabinet tonight. We'll see if there is something in there that we don't know about.'

So a fresh plate was put in the chemical cabinet. The door was closed for the night.

In the morning the two men hurried to the cabinet. Anxiously they opened it and took out the plate. Bewildered, they looked at it. The plate was developed. But the cupboard was empty.

'Well, this is strange', said Daguerre. 'We must search this cabinet. There is something in here that we do not know about. A plate can't develop itself.' Sure enough, after a thorough search, they found that some mercury had been spilled: on one of the shelves. Mercury, that must be the developer Daguerre was looking for. At once he put some mercury on an exposed plate. And to his delight, he found that it was a good developing agent. It brought

44 *Reading to learn*

out the lights and shadows just as they were in nature. At last he had succeeded. This meant that he could now make photographs.

Photography still had a long way to go before it reached the state it is in today. But that spilled mercury in Daguerre's chemical cabinet gave it a big push forward by providing the essential developing agent.

Questions

1 Which chemical did Daguerre discover to be a good developing agent for photographs?
2 How did he discover this agent?
3 What sort of a personality do you think Daguerre possessed?
4 Do you think Daguerre made his discovery in an efficient, scientific way?
5 Do you think the author makes it clear how Daguerre decided it must be something other than the last bottle which was responsible for developing the plate?
6 What do you think of this passage from the point of view of a person seeking information for a 'topic' on photography?

(The answers are given at the end of the chapter.)

The purpose of this activity is to develop your ability to recognise fairly quickly, and before you actually start reading, the kind of operations you need to perform on a text. That in turn will help you to choose the right reading tactics. Now all this may seem very slow and cumbersome, especially when you do it for the first time. When you have done it several times you will find that you speed up very considerably. Your aim should be for it to become almost automatic. The key points to remember are: 1) whenever you read to learn begin by specifying your reading purposes; 2) relate your purposes to the skills necessary to achieve them – and so to the reading tactics and strategies you need to employ.

It may help you to think about reading purposes in terms of *command words*. The next activity shows you how to set about this.

Using command words to specify purpose

Command words, in this context, are words like 'find', 'criticise', 'discuss', 'compare' and 'summarise' which direct you to perform certain operations with respect to the text. They are often found in examination questions, and they are useful when it comes to relating reading purpose to comprehension skills. Some command words tend to be regularly associated with particular skills or operations, and when you have thought through the associations you will probably remember some of the links and this will serve as a kind of shortcut in carrying out the operations described in this chapter. Be warned, however: you cannot rely rigidly on the associations. They are only a guide.

Table 3.2 lists fifty command words which commonly occur in questions relating to reading purposes. They are shown as a column down the left-hand side. They indicate the kind of operations a reader is expected to perform. The table also lists categories used in describing a text. These are shown as a row across the top. We discuss these categories in a later chapter but you will be able to relate the terms to ones you have already met in Table 3.1. There they related to sets of comprehension sub-skills which themselves were grouped under the five broad headings of literal (1); reorganisation, analysis and synthesis (2); appreciation (3); evaluation (4) and extrapolation (5). The headings correspond to different levels in the taxonomy and are numbered in ascending order of abstraction.

Table 3.2 shows how one student, Jane, related eighteen command words to different levels of the taxonomy when she was carrying out a reading assignment. She had previously thought through her purposes and constructed a purpose hierarchy, expressing her purposes in the form of command words. She then surveyed the text she was concerned with, noting generally in her mind the features of the text which corresponded roughly to the categories listed across the top of Table 3.2. Then, bearing in mind both the text and her purposes, she assigned each of the command words she had derived to a level in the taxonomy.

For example, 'find', 'identify' and 'list' related to *Literal* (1) and to 'details', 'instructions' and 'main points' in the text so she put a (1) in the appropriate square. 'Judge', 'appraise', 'review' and 'compare' related to *Evaluation* (4) and to 'sequence', 'main ideas',

46   *Reading to learn*

Table 3.2

Commands or operations relating to specific reading purposes (rows) × A structural description of the contents of a text (columns)

Command	Facts	Details, e.g. examples, quantities	Sequence (logical)	Sequence (temporal)	Cause and effect	Specifics	Elements	Concepts	Generalisations	Main ideas	Main points	Relationships between specifics	Ways of dealing with specifics, e.g. paraphrase	Principles – theories	Universals and abstractions	Relationships between concepts	Evaluations	Extrapolations	Signposts	Instructions
Survey																				
Examine																				
Explore																				
Memorise								1												
Know																				
Evaluate																				
Analyse																2				
Infer																				
Summarise									2											
Recognise					1															
Recall																				
Appreciate																				
Extrapolate																				
Translate																				
Synthesise																				
Apply																				
Interpret																2			2	
Identify										1										
Construct									5											
Arrange																				
Locate																				
Select															2					
Outline																				
Find	1																			
Create																				
Respond					3	1														
Value																				
Organise																				
Reason																				
Demonstrate																				
Remember																				
Judge									4											
Discriminate																				

Table 3.2 – continued

Commands or operations relating to specific reading purposes	A structural description of the contents of a text	Facts	Details, e.g. examples, quantities sequence (logical)	Sequence (temporal)	Cause and effect	Specifics	Elements	Concepts	Generalisations	Main ideas	Main points	Relationships between specifics	Ways of dealing with specifics, e.g. paraphrase	Principles – theories	Universals and abstractions	Relationships between concepts	Evaluations	Extrapolations	Signposts	Instructions
Deduce																				
Assess		3																		
Create																		5		2
Consider																				
Discuss																				
Conjecture																				
Describe																				
Explain																				
List																		2		I
Represent																				
Hypothesise																				
Appraise			4																	
Criticise																				
Review																4				
Precis																				
Discover		I																3		
Compare		2														4				
Invent																		5		2

Note. Numbers 1–5 represent categories in the purpose taxonomy (Table 3.1).

'principles and theories' and 'relationships between concepts' so she entered (4) in those squares.

After she had performed this exercise with one or two different texts she could see that certain command words normally relate to certain levels in the taxonomy: 'criticise' with *evaluation*, 'construct' with *extrapolation*, and 'list' with *literal*, for example. Once she had thought this through she was able to use this knowledge as a short cut to identifying the skills a particular text required her to use.

However, the exercise also brought home to her the fact that she

48 *Reading to learn*

had to use this knowledge flexibly. She found, for example, that one command word, 'memorise', required her to perform the same kind of mental operation (*literal*) on two different parts of the text, 'Concepts' and 'universals and abstractions', while another command word, 'compare', demanded different operations (*reorganisation* and *evaluation*) on two different parts of the text, 'details' and 'relationships between concepts'. Yet again, two different command words, e.g. 'analyse' and 'interpret', may demand the same kind of comprehension skill (*reorganisation*) on the same part of the text, 'relationship between concepts', or, as with 'summarise' and 'identify', a different kind of comprehension (e.g. 'reorganisation' and *literal*) on the same part of a text, 'Main points'. Even so, there are consistent patterns.

Activity 3.4   **Using command words to relate purpose to text**

The purpose of this activity is to help you to relate reading purposes to the text by using command words. As with all activities the intention is to get you to think about reading to learn in more precise terms than you would otherwise do. In this way you come to control the process more. When you first try this activity you will probably do it very slowly. It doesn't matter. At this stage what is important is that you should think the process through. If you then repeat the activity two or three times you will find that the general lines of the approach sink in and the whole process speeds up. You will probably find that you develop your own shortcuts. Remember the overall aim is to develop your ability to specify reading purposes more and more precisely, and increasingly in terms of what you have to do to the text to achieve them.

Procedure

1 *Choose a text* which you hope to learn something from by reading. A section from a textbook would be fine.
2 *Survey the text*, bearing roughly in mind the categories listed across the top of Table 3.2. We shall return to these categories in our next chapter and then you will find it easier to remember them. At this point all you are trying to do is to get an idea of the nature

of the text, its breakdown into factual material, theoretical material, introduction, conclusions and so on.

3 Construct your own purpose hierarchy for the text, referring to the list of command words as you think about the lower order, more detailed, purposes. For example, some of your purposes expressed in the form of commands might be

Memorise details of dates
Identify the author's main points
Criticise his account
Summarise his argument

4 Refer your list of commands to the purpose taxonomy (Table 3.1) and classify the comprehension level required.

What this should leave you with is a clearer idea of the nature of the operations you need to perform on the text in order to achieve your reading purposes. Later this will help you to identify appropriate reading tactics and strategies. It may even be possible for you already to cast your mind back to the previous chapter and be able to say something about the tactics you might employ. It does not matter at this stage if you can't. The important thing is that you should be breaking rough, general aims down into hard, specific reading purposes.

When you have finished the exercise stand back from it in your mind and mentally review both your purposes and the comprehension skills that go with them. In time all this should be done mentally – and automatically.

It may be of interest to you to construct a grid of the type shown in Table 3.2 and to enter your classification on it. This will underline the relationship between purposes and different parts of the text.

Summary

This chapter has been a complex one, and the way of thinking about reading purposes that we have presented may seem cumbersome. Our aim has been to provide the reader with sufficient material to allow him to come at purposes from a variety of directions. To a certain extent the reader can pick and choose.

50   *Reading to learn*

The important thing to bear in mind is the point of the exercises. They are intended to increase awareness of the operation which the reader is required to perform on the text as he or she reads it. Sometimes he may be identifying details; at other times he may be evaluating principles or making inferences. The reader will find that over a period of time he or she will develop an ability to recognise quickly the operations and skills that particular texts and particular purposes require. Initially, though, the whole business of purpose identification may seem abstract, laborious and, indeed, redundant. It is worth persevering, however. Time spent on talking oneself through one's reading purposes is time well spent. Purpose specification is often the key to efficient reading. Too often the door remains locked because the key is never used.

Answers to Activity 3.3   Question purposes clarified

1 Literal comprehension. Recall of a particular detail, explicitly stated in the passage.
2 Recognition of a sequence and organising the passage into outline form in a condensed way. This requires *both* literal recognition of a sequence and reorganisation.
3 Inference of character traits; this question requires the reader to hypothesise about the nature of the personality. The clues, however, are not explicitly presented, hence extrapolation. It also tests the reader's evaluation of the character. There is an overlap here.
4 Evaluation of behaviour of main character by comparison of own ideas and these details provided by the author.
5 Judgement of adequacy of text but requiring also a literal recall of a detail in a sequence of details.
6 Evaluation and appreciation of the whole passage.

4
Reading for meaning

Overview

The way you read a text depends in part upon your purpose. If, for instance, you are reading for factual information you will use different tactics and strategies from those you would employ if your purpose were to grasp a theory. But are you sure what is theory and what is fact? Our aim in this chapter is to help you to make distinctions more confidently. In particular we want to sharpen your sense of what is the main idea of a text, what are elaborations and applications of it, and what are qualifications of and objections to it. We approach this by trying to make you more aware of the cues which authors conveniently put in the text to guide you. As in the case of reading tactics, strategies and purposes it helps to have some sort of record which exhibits your thinking. We put forward an idea for one such record in the form of a flow diagram. In the next chapter we show how by comparing a flow diagram of a particular text with a record of the way you read the text it is possible to develop your reading effectiveness. However, as in the previous chapters, it is important to remember that the techniques are merely a means to an end, and the end in this case is to increase your awareness of the nature of the text you are reading.

Activity 4.1   **Mapping meaning**

Choose a fairly academic text. Again, a section or chapter from a textbook would be suitable. Equip yourself with several coloured pencils. Go through the text underlining, *theories, definitions,*

52 *Reading to learn*

examples, main ideas, details, procedures. Use a different colour for each category.

The pattern of colour will tell you something about the nature of the text: it will tell you what kind of text it is (heavily theoretical, densely factual) and also how the different categories are distributed through the text. Give yourself a reading to learn purpose and ask yourself how you would approach the text in terms of reading tactics and strategies. What part of the text would you concentrate on?Now give yourself a different reading purpose and ask yourself what parts of the text are relevant to that.

Now look at the pattern of colour overall. What can you say about the way the text is organised (does it, for instance, begin with theory, then give examples; or work up to a theory via examples?).

Finally, think over your reasons for putting items in different categories. If you are doing this in a group, discussion with others can be valuable at this point. In any case it may be interesting to compare your colour map with that of your neighbour. If you cannot agree on the main idea of the passage, this could be telling you something about your reading to learn skills (or those of your neighbour, of course!).

To be able to give a theoretical justification for placing one item in one category and one in another may involve the use of quite sophisticated skills. Our purpose here is recognition, and discussion should be directed to that end. Our experience is that a considerable number of first-year undergraduates are uncertain about what is fact and what theory, what inference and what opinion. Activity 4.1 could, therefore, have a general use. In the particular context of reading to learn, however, we can draw on aids which are not properly part of a philosophical discussion. Nearly all authors give us cues as to how we are to take parts of the text.

Reading cues

Reading cues are as it were signposts planted by the author to tell the reader how to get at the content of the text. They begin before

Reading for meaning 53

you come to the text proper. The title, and often more specifically, the sub-title, tell you what the book is about. The table of contents goes into more detail. And, of course, the index goes into more detail still. Often in reading to learn a good place to start reading is the end, and this is particularly true when you are confronted with a formidable tome of a book. The publisher's blurb on the jacket usually gives some idea of the level at which the subject is treated, and it is often worth looking at the date of publication, especially with scientific books, to check that they are not out of date. Reading these two things first can save you wasting your time.

Another set of signposts that can save time is built into the way the text is set out. Many scientific articles are prefaced by an abstract, which conveniently condenses the argument of the article. Those that don't have an abstract usually summarise their argument at the end and present their conclusions. It is not so much that if you read the abstract or the conclusions you don't need to read the article itself (although that may be true); rather it is that reading them may direct your attention to the particular parts of the text which you are interested in.

Many textbooks also preface their chapters with an introductory survey of content and end them with a summary of what has been said. Often the chapter is broken into sections, each with a heading signposting content. Important points are sometimes printed in italics or emphasised in some other way.

All these are fairly obvious; but what is often overlooked are the signposts buried in the text itself. There are signposts that tell the reader where he is going ('I shall discuss the theory of . . .'), signposts that tell the reader where he is coming from ('I have already presented the main principles . . .') and signposts along the route ('My next point is . . .'). More subtle are the signposts which point to the ways in which parts of the text are to be taken: 'The inferences are clear' (they are inferences not facts); 'There is a circularity in this proposition' (the proposition may be of interest but it is not one to be seriously advanced); 'To summarise the main ideas' (fairly accepted principles); 'My own feelings are . . .' (this is opinion – but it may be soundly based) and 'Put this another way:' (a restatement, and so logically equivalent to the passage being restated).

When one looks at a text it is surprising how many words and phrases act as signposts. Here are some examples:

54 *Reading to learn*

Consider the following points . . . I must stress . . . Remember . . .
In my opinion . . . Little is known about . . . Moreover . . . Since
. . . Anyway . . . The argument is important . . . You will see that
what I am building up to is the proposition that . . . etc.

There are so many that one cannot list them all. They are dotted
about everywhere in a text, and academic texts are full of them.
Activity 4.2 is intended to begin the process of making you more
aware of them.

Activity 4.2 Identifying signpost phrases

Choose a fairly lengthy text, such as an article or a chapter in a
book. Read it through and note the signpost phrases.

Once you have begun to be aware of such author cues you will find
it easy to spot them when you are reading, and this will help your
reading a great deal.

Access cues and context cues

The cues we have been talking about tell us how to approach a text.
They are *access* cues. They tell us where certain things are and how
we are to take them. But the ability to arrive at the meaning of a text
involves being sensitive to another kind of cue as well. Each word,
phrase or sentence in a text derives its meaning partly from its
context. Other words and phrases in the passage help us to
understand their meaning. They work, that is, as cues to meaning.
We will call this kind of cue a *context* cue. Activity 4.3 will help you
to see what we mean.

Activity 4.3 Using context cues to find meanings

Complete the passage below by putting the missing words in the

Reading for meaning 55

blanks. Check your answers against those given in the left hand margin. The missing words are printed backwards. We have included the first letters of some of the missing words to give you an additional cue.

The airport

syawnur

sgnidliub
rewot
gnivirra
gnitraped
senalp
deriaper
letoh
sesub
sregnessap
dnuorg
esilaer
senihcam
yvaeh

An airport is a very busy place. Besides the long   needed by planes when coming in to land or when taking off, there are many important   on it. These are all near one another, and the most important one is the control t   from which signals by wireless are made to a   and d   planes. There are

also hangars where   are kept until they are needed and where they can be overhauled and r   , waiting-rooms for passengers, customs offices, restaurants, and very often a   . If the airport is some distance from a town or railway station,   may be provided for the convenience of   . One has to see on the   a place used for Trans-Atlantic or Continental flights to   how big these   are, and what   loads they can carry.

The main point about this activity is how easy it is to find words that will fit. This is because the other words in the passage work so effectively as cues. Even when key words are left out you can arrive at their meaning simply by responding to the cues available in the rest of the passage.

Some of the omissions can be supplied by relying on textual content. For others, however, you have to rely more on your own knowledge. We can see them both as context cues, but in one case the context is on the page, whereas in the other case it is in the head. The latter is especially important for the kind of reading you have to do when studying at an advanced level, and the presence of this kind of knowledge is one of the things that distinguishes the advanced reader from the child beginning to read.

Within the text there are two major kinds of cues that can help

56 *Reading to learn*

readers to anticipate words or phrases. They are syntactic cues (ones to do with grammar) and semantic cues (cues to do with meaning). Our working knowledge of syntax and grammar and our experience of sentence structure usually enables us to anticipate the particular parts of speech that will follow previous words in a sentence. In the sentence 'The cat sat on the mat' 'cat' and 'mat' are nouns. Words following 'the' are usually nouns or adjectives. You don't have to know this consciously. The knowledge you have somehow deep down which enables you to speak grammatically usually tells you when a word is the right kind of word to be used in a particular place.

Semantic cues are also very powerful. Take, for example, the sentence 'He could travel either by bus or by car, and, as his car had broken down, he went by   .' The meaning of the context tells us that there are only two alternatives and that one is unusable. This cues us to anticipate the other alternative, i.e. bus.

We can look upon syntactic cues and semantic cues as operating to reduce the number of possible meanings that an unknown word or phrase may have, and so making it more probable that we shall predict the right word when we come to it in a passage. Some writers, as was pointed out in the first chapter, see reading as involving a continuous process of predicting words. If the anticipated meanings match with the words and sentences on the page, the reader reads on. If they mismatch he or she becomes aware of misunderstanding, and if he or she is skilled the strategy is reorganised in an attempt to correct this. According to this view, the ability to anticipate is fundamental to good reading and, since sensitivity to context cues contributes crucially to this, so does our ability to identify and respond to them.

The following table shows you the kind of cues operating in the passage you have just completed. Column 1 lists the missing words, column 2 says whether the cues are semantic or syntactic. The operation of cues may depend on searching backwards or forwards in the text. Column 3 classifies the cues as FA (forward-acting) or BA (backward-acting). Column 4 tells you whether the text cues are local to the sentence (within) or operate across sentences (across). Column 5 classifies the cues according to whether they depend on text content (TC) or reader's knowledge (RK). (We argue that there are *no* cues depending just on reader's knowledge here. It can all be worked out from the text. You may not agree!)

Reading for meaning 57

Table 4.1 Classification of the important context cues used in 'The airport'

Runways	semantic	FA	within	TC
buildings	semantic	FA	across	TC
tower	semantic	BA	within	TC
arriving	semantic	BA	within	TC
departing	semantic	BA	within	TC
planes	syntactic	BA	within	TC
repaired	semantic	BA	within	TC
hotel	syntactic	BA	within	TC
buses	syntactic	BA	within	TC
passengers	syntactic	BA	within	TC
ground	semantic	FA	within	TC
realise	syntactic	FA	within	TC
machines	syntactic	BA	within	TC
heavy	semantic	FA	within	TC

Activity 4.4   **Classifying context cues**

The purpose of this activity is to increase your awareness of context cues and make you a little more conscious of the way they operate. Read the passage which follows, filling in the blanks. For each of your words write down

a whether the cuing is syntactic or semantic;
b whether it is forward or backward acting;
c whether it operates within the sentence or across sentences;
d whether it relies on text content or reader's knowledge.

Extract from Heinrich Harrer's 'Seven Years in Tibet'

My favourite expedition was to a   mountain lake a short day's march   Lhasa. The first time I went   was during the rainy season, when   was feared that the waters would   and flood the town. According to   ancient legend this lake is connected   a subterranean channel with an underground   said to exist beneath the cathedral.   year the Government used to send   to propitiate the spirits of the   with prayers and offerings. Pilgrims, too,   to go there and throw rings

58   *Reading to learn*

coins into the water. By the	stood a few stone huts in	one
could find shelter. I found	the lake did not threaten the	
of the town in the slightest	. Even if it had overflowed, no	
would have been done. It was	peaceful, idyllic place.	

In the Appendix to this chapter we give the words the author used, together with an analysis of the relevant context cues. You may find it interesting to compare the analysis with your own classification and also, if you are doing this activity in a group, to discuss whether you agree with particular judgements. We have found that discussion does improve people's scores. However, the point of the exercise is not that you should become good at classifying but that your awareness of context cues and of the way they operate should be heightened.

Using a flow diagram to map meaning

A good reader does not usually read a text through from beginning to end. He or she refers backwards and forwards in search of meaning. This may be because the author's 'signposts' refer the reader specifically to another part of the text. It may be because the reader's purpose makes only some parts of the text relevant. Or it may be that the reader is unconsciously or semi-consciously seeking context cues. Often when a good reader is reading an academic text a kind of inner conversation goes on. 'Is this another main point or is it an example?' 'How does this relate to what the author has just said?' 'I don't follow the flow of argument from A to B. Let's look at it again.'

The reader, in his search for meaning, constantly needs to refer from one part of the text to another. He needs, that is, to be aware of the relationships between the different parts of the text, to know what *is* a main point and what an example or a sub-point.

Our next activity is designed to increase the reader's awareness of these relationships. Again, our method is to suggest a way of recording the way a reader perceives the relationships. If what goes on in the reader's head is externalised, he or she can look at it more objectively than might otherwise be the case and perhaps criticise and improve it. The object, we stress, is not to produce the record,

Reading for meaning 59

but to develop awareness. The record, and the exercise, is merely a means to that end.

One way of displaying relationships is by means of a flow diagram. You may already be familiar with this from your own studies, but it is unlikely that you will have applied the technique to a piece of prose so we will take you through the technique as if you had not previously tried it. Let us begin by taking an example. Consider the following sentence:

> Owing to this struggle, variations, however slight and from whatever cause proceeding, if they be in any degree profitable to the individuals of a species in their infinitely complex relation to other organic beings and to their physical conditions of life, will tend to the preservation of such individuals and will generally be inherited by the offspring.

This sentence, which is taken from Darwin's *Origin of Species*, is quite a complex one, and in extracting its meaning one may be forgiven if one pauses over the relationship of some of the phrases to each other. Even for a passage consisting of only one sentence a flow diagram may be helpful.

The first thing we need to do is to divide the sentence up into smaller units of meaning.

1 Owing to this struggle,
2 variations, however slight and from whatever cause proceeding,
3 if they be in any degree profitable to the individuals of a species
4 in their infinitely complex relation to other organic beings and to their physical conditions of life,
5 will tend to the preservation of such individuals
6 and will generally be inherited by the offspring.

The next thing to do is to think about each unit and put it in one of the following categories: main theme, qualification, and link. By qualification is meant something which tells you more about the main theme but is not itself part of the main theme. It provides additional information about the items in the main theme. By link we mean a phrase which links one part of the passage to another. Thus 'Owing to this struggle' links the sentence we are considering to previous sentences which have described the struggle.

It is helpful to think about the categories in terms of columns. If you take a piece of paper and divide it into three columns, heading

60   *Reading to learn*

Figure 4.1   Using a flow diagram to map meaning

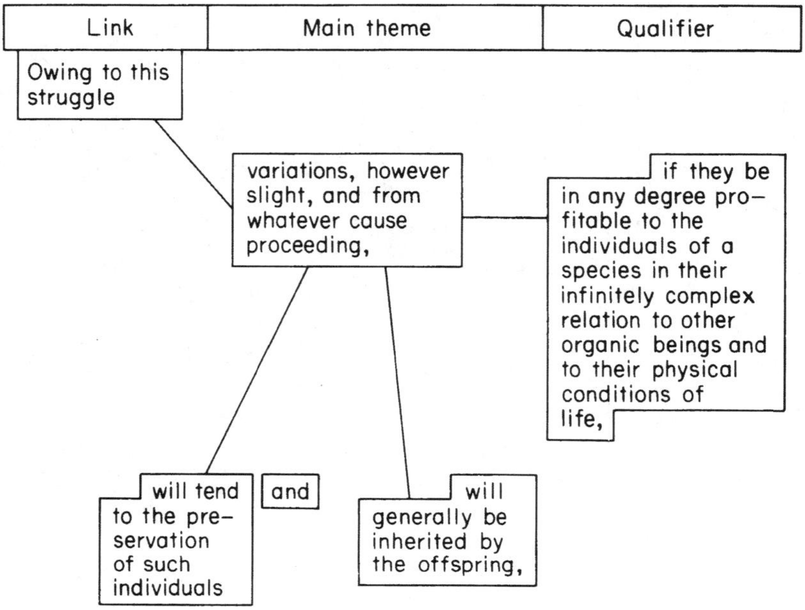

Link	Main theme	Qualifier

Owing to this struggle

variations, however slight, and from whatever cause proceeding,

if they be in any degree pro— fitable to the individuals of a species in their infinitely complex relation to other organic beings and to their physical conditions of life,

will tend to the pre— servation of such individuals

and

will generally be inherited by the offspring,

the left-hand one *Link,* the middle one *Main theme,* and the right-hand one *Qualification,* as in Fig. 4.1 above, you can then ask yourself of each item in which column it should go. Thus the first item, 'Owing to this struggle', is a link and goes in the left-hand column.

The advantage of presenting the material in this way is that it becomes possible to exhibit the connections between the items by drawing lines or arrows. We then get a diagram of the way the meaning flows.

Fig. 4.1 above sets out one way of showing relationships between the items in the sentence that we are considering. You will see that we have boxed items 3 and 4 together. Both qualify what we see as the main theme, which is the relationship between the variations and what they will do.

It is possible to box items together or divide them up into smaller boxes. If you do the latter you can describe the meaning in more detail. Thus you may have been bothered by our including 'however slight and from whatever cause proceeding' with 'variations' in the first place. 'However slight and from whatever cause proceeding' is itself a qualification of 'variations' and really consists of two separate propositions, one about slightness and one about cause. But that does not matter. It can all be shown by further boxes and further arrows, as in Fig. 4.2, which maps the flow of meaning at a more detailed level.

In constructing this particular flow diagram three categories (*link*, *main theme* and *qualification*) were enough. When, as is usually

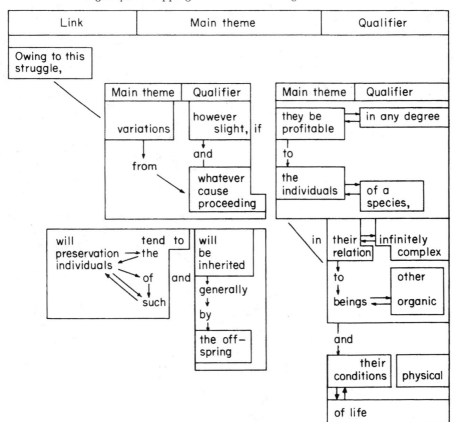

Figure 4.2 Mapping the flow of meaning at a more detailed level

the case, one is concerned with texts longer than just one sentence it is useful to add a fourth, *elaboration*. By *elaboration* is meant the addition of further, incidental detail. The distinction between qualification and elaboration is confined to the addition of further detail, such as examples, dates, names, quantities, analogies and descriptive matter. It does not matter if initially your classification is rather tentative. Be prepared to adjust it as you go along. At least it will give you a framework with which to approach the text. If you need to you can refine it later.

Once you have grasped the principle, incidentally, you may wish to change or amplify the categories. Some science students differentiated the main theme category into *review of theory*, *evaluation of theory*, and *inferences*. Some English students introduced categories such as imagery, sound patterns and so on.

Let us recapitulate the procedure:

Constructing a flow diagram of a text
1 Read the text to get an overview of the range of meaning.
2 Divide the text up into smaller units. (In an extended text you can usually take paragraphs as your unit.) Number each unit.
3 Consider each unit carefully and decide whether it forms part of the main theme or whether it qualifies or elaborates it.
4 Divide a piece of paper into three (or four if you think it advisable) columns, heading the first column *Link*, the second *Main theme*, the third *Qualification* and the fourth, if you have one, *Elaboration*. When you have decided which column is for a particular unit, draw a box in the column and put in it the number you have given the unit (to save you writing out all the words again as we have done, in the interests of clarity, in Figs. 4.1 and 4.2). Do this for each unit.
5 Indicate with arrows how each unit relates to the others.
6 Check the units in the main theme column by reading them in sequence. Does this pull out the meaning?

Now that you have an idea what a flow diagram is and are acquainted with the procedure for constructing one which can be applied to mapping the flow of meaning in a text, we can proceed to try the technique out in practice. The activity which follows is designed to make you more aware of the connections of meaning within a text.

Reading for meaning 63

Activity 4.5 **Mapping the meaning of a paragraph by means of a flow diagram**

The paragraph below has been written deliberately in a complicated way. You are unlikely to come across many paragraphs of this length and complexity in your reading. To help you we have suggested a breakdown into meaning units. Each number down the left-hand margin indicates one unit of meaning. Thus the first three lines taken together form one unit (1); the fourth line by itself forms another unit (2); similarly with the fifth and sixth lines (3); lines 7, 8 and 9 combine to form one unit only (4), and so on.

Using the categories *Link*, *Main theme*, *Qualification* and *Elaboration*, prepare a flow diagram of the paragraph.

1   The idea of charting the meaning of a text in the form of a flow diagram has been introduced in a number of reading to learn activities.

2   You are encouraged to use the flow diagram as a referent

3   against which to assess your reading outcome. On page 61 you are shown how to prepare flow diagrams.

4   People working with the flow diagram technique have found that the exercise of clearly describing their own understanding of a text helps them to check and improve it.

5   By the time you have drawn a flow diagram of this paragraph, you may well find there is more to it than your first cursory reading led

6   you to surmise. When a number of people each draw a flow diagram of the same text, comparison reveals key areas of agreement or disagreement.

7   Comparison of flow diagrams is made much easier if everybody uses the same conventions.

8   Discussion about areas of disagreement can reveal one of two things: either the readers have approached the text with different purposes or if their purposes are similar their understandings are different.

9   When discussion is focused in this way it is possible for informed people to agree on purposes and arrive at a common flow diagram.

10 The 'objectivity' of such a description is no more than a shared subjectivity among the participants.

11 When the participants can reasonably be judged to be both competent readers and experts in the subject matter, their agreed

64 *Reading to learn*

flow diagram can be used as a referent against which the reading of other people can be evaluated.

12 An agreed flow diagram can be used as a basis for evaluating either a reading outcome or interpreting a reading record.

13 As we have seen in the earlier reading to learn activities, the agreed flow diagram can be used as a map against which the reader's description of what he has learnt can be assessed.

14 Another reason for describing the meaning structure of a text in the form of a flow diagram is to explore how the record obtained by the observer can be interpreted in the light of the purpose of the reader to reveal a pattern of interaction with the text which may or may not result in the reading outcomes which he is seeking.

15 The flow diagram can therefore be used in two major ways. The
16 individual reader can describe the meaning of the text to himself and by externalising this structure of meaning, he can check and improve his understanding.

17 When informed people, or even the author, can provide their version, it can be used as a referent against which other readers' understandings can be reviewed.

When you have completed your diagram turn to the Appendix at the end of the chapter and compare it with ours.

Usually, texts will not be as hard to analyse as this one. You will find that texts which are rather longer and consist of several paragraphs are on the whole much easier to produce a flow diagram for. Try it with a section from a textbook, or this book. Use paragraphs as the units for analysis. The flow diagram on p. 103 shows how this can be done. Because textbooks normally 'signpost' content heavily it will be easier for you to find your way around in a text. Repeat this activity two or three times with texts of that sort and you will probably find that you can reduce your flow diagram to a quick sketch with numbers on the back of an envelope. With a little more practice you will need to use the technique only with texts of exceptional difficulty.

The flow diagram technique has a variety of uses. Used together with a purpose hierarchy, for example, it indicates the parts of a text relevant to specific reading purposes. Used in conjunction with

Reading for meaning 65

the read record it can throw light on whether your reading tactics are engaging appropriately with the various parts of the text. (We will show you how this can be done in the next chapter.) Used by itself the technique can be a helpful way of clarifying the meaning of a passage. It also provides a good basis for organising notes, for planning and writing essays, and for editing and restructuring a piece of your own writing.

Summary

Our aim here has been to use it to develop the reader's awareness of the relationships of ideas within a text. We spoke earlier of the kind of conversation that a good reader holds with himself about a text. As he reads he asks himself questions like 'Is this another main point or is it an example?' 'I've missed the connection; how does this lead to that?' 'I don't quite get the meaning. Has he said something about this earlier on which would help?' The point of using the flow diagram technique in the way we have done is to help you develop the ability to hold such a conversation. Flow diagrams are merely a ladder which should be kicked away when you have reached your goal.

There are, of course, other techniques for promoting logical awareness but we have suggested the flow diagram one because it has a number of incidental advantages. It presents meaning in the form of a visual record which, as we mentioned above, can be set beside other visual records such as the read record. It is also a good technique for use by two people or by a group. There is a real gain in comparing your flow diagram of a passage with someone else's and discussing differences. Discussion of this sort can help to develop awareness, but for it to be fruitful it needs a basis to proceed on, which the flow diagram can provide.

66   *Reading to learn*

Appendix 4.1 Analysis of contextual cues (Activity 4.4)

Correct response	Syn/Sem	FA/BA	within/ across	TC/RK
little	sem	BA	w	TC
from	sem	FA/BA	a	TC
there	sem	FA	a	TC
it	syn	BA	w	TC
overflow	sem	BA	w/a	TC
an	syn	BA	w	TC
by	syn	FA	w	TC
lake	sem	FA	w	TC
Every	sem	BA	w	TC
monks	sem	BA	w	RK
lake	sem	BA	w	TC
used	syn	FA	w	TC
and	syn	BA	w	TC
lake	sem	BA	a	TC
which	syn	BA	w	TC
that	syn	BA	w	TC
safety	sem	BA	a	TC
degree	sem	FA	w	TC
harm	sem	BA	a	TC
a	syn	BA	w	TC

Reading for meaning

Appendix 4.2 Flow diagram of paragraph in Activity 4.5

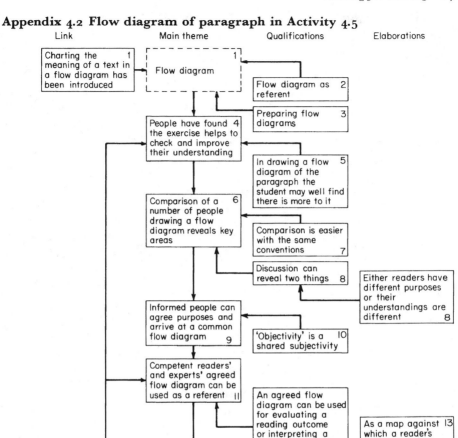

5
Meaning and strategy

Overview

In this chapter our aim is to introduce you to the idea of using flow diagrams and read records together to tell you something about how you are approaching a text. In Chapter 7 we shall go into this in more detail but it may be helpful to you to have a preliminary look at the approach at this point. By comparing our read record for a particular passage with our flow diagram of the same passage we may be able to find out whether our reading tactic was correctly chosen and whether the read itself was appropriately tailored to the passage. To keep things simple we shall restrict ourselves in this chapter to the sentence level.

Reading behaviour and flow diagrams

By setting a read record for a particular text beside a flow diagram for the text one can learn something about the way in which the reader approached the passage. Suppose, for example, that the record shows that the reader stopped on lines x and y and made notes; and suppose that x and y map onto the *Elaboration* column of the flow diagram. What can we infer? The presumption is that the reader was seeking detailed information. If that was not his purpose, if, for instance, he was trying to select the main idea of the passage, then his approach has gone sadly astray.

To find out if that was his purpose we would need to ask him. The read record and the flow diagram will not give us that information. What they can do, and do particularly well if used together, is to provide us with data which will enable us to be more precise in our questions. They are aids only. At the end of the day, if we ourselves are the reader, we have to rely on our own awareness. The techniques are means of developing that awareness.

Meaning and strategy 69

To see how the read record and the flow diagram combined can give us added information let us take an example. And as in the last chapter let us take as our example that long sentence from Darwin's *Origin of Species* (it is given again overleaf).

GARETH'S READING STRATEGY

Fig. 5.1 shows the overall read record of a sixth form biology student, Gareth, reading the sentence. As can be seen from the diagram, he read the sentence four times. Each read, if you remember, is taken as one tactic. The four reads taken together show his overall strategy for reading the passage.

As we see from Fig. 5.1(a), Gareth's first tactic was a smooth read. Fig. 5.1(b) shows the read plotted alongside the sentence itself. The sentence was set out one word to a line so that when the reader read it using a viewing window an observer could plot the track he followed, exactly as if he were reading a longer passage line by line. The read was then plotted on a piece of graph paper in the way shown in Chapter 2. The horizontal axis shows time taken and the vertical axis shows position in text as measured by word number (there are 57 words in the sentence, so the track rises from word 1 to word 57). We can see from the read record that Gareth read the sentence smoothly and without any stopping or backtracking.

We have also divided the sentence, as before, into units of meaning to assist us in constructing a flow diagram. In Fig. 5.1(b) the units of meaning are indicated by the numbers down the left-hand side of the sentence (1 to 6). These are shown as boxes with numbers in Fig. 5.1(c).

Fig. 5.1(c) sets units of meaning alongside a read. In this case the read record we have taken is the second one and, as we can see, it shows that Gareth adopted an 'item read' tactic for this part of his strategy. We can see that the track is much more broken than it was in the case of the smooth read. Gareth is proceeding steadily through the passage dwelling on each part of the sentence in turn. Only once is there any real backtrack. There is no real difference in the ways he treats the units of meaning. Whether they are main ideas or illustrations they are all treated in the same way in an item read.

The same is not true, however, when Gareth reads the sentence for the third time. His third tactic is a search read. This time he is

70 *Reading to learn*

Figure 5.1 (a) Overall sentence read

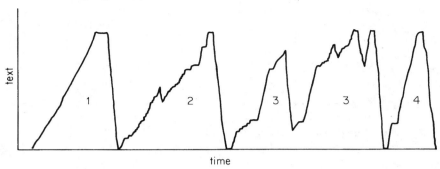

Note. 1,2,3,4 = read tactics

(b) Tactic 1 – a smooth read

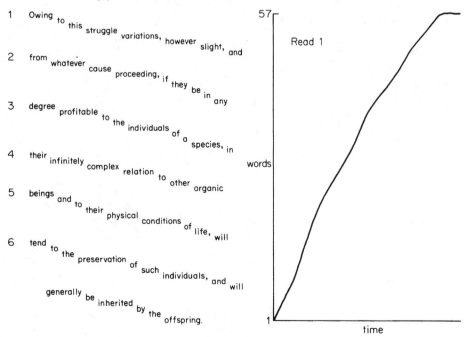

Meaning and strategy 71

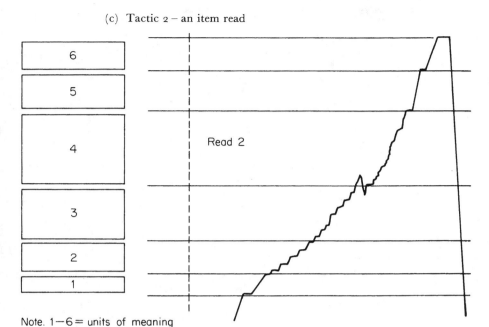

(c) Tactic 2 – an item read

Note. 1—6 = units of meaning

searching backwards and forwards through the sentence trying to find the relationships between particular units of meaning. Fig. 5.1(d) shows the read alongside the flow diagram of the sentence. We see from this that Gareth began fairly steadily with units 1 and 2 but then, spotting that unit 2 was part of the main theme and related to unit 5, he shot ahead to glance at that part of the sentence, and then returned to fit the rest in. This was sense because units 3 and 4 are essentially elaboration of the main theme – as we can tell by glancing at the flow diagram.

For his fourth read Gareth went back to a smooth read, though as we saw in Chapter 2 he might have been employing it for a different purpose than was the case when he read the sentence for the first time. Notice, though, the break in the read at the end of unit 2. Referring to the flow diagram may provide an explanation (Fig. 5.1(e)).

Let us go back now and talk through Gareth's strategy as a whole. He was reading the book to find out about Darwin's theory of natural selection. He came upon this sentence and found it a

72 *Reading to learn*

(d) Tactic 3 – a search read

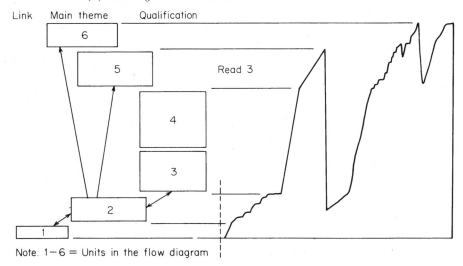

Note. 1–6 = Units in the flow diagram

(e) Tactic 4 – a smooth read

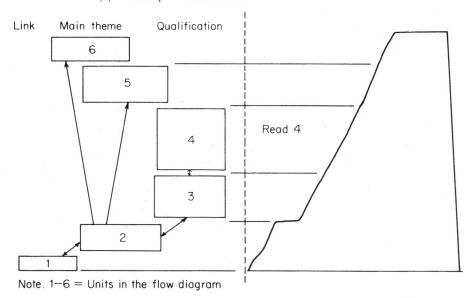

Note. 1–6 = Units in the flow diagram

Meaning and strategy 73

rather complex, difficult one. His specific reading purpose at this point was to *identify* and *abstract* the main idea. He adopted a particular strategy for reading the sentence. As we have seen, it comprised four separate reads.

In read 1 Gareth was trying to get an overview of the sentence but he found this quite difficult. However, he did not let this slow him down, as the record shows.

In read 2 he decided to break the sentence up into smaller units of meaning that he could handle more easily. Notice that although he reads linearly he does pay more attention to units 2, 3 and 4. Gareth reported afterwards that he was trying to sort out the key phrase and later decided to allocate 3 and 4 as *not* main theme but qualification.

In read 3 he searched backwards and forwards in an attempt to work out the logical structure of the sentence and so get at the main idea – which was, of course, the purpose he had set himself. By comparing the flow diagram with the record for this read one can see that Gareth was connecting units 2, 5 and 6 together in his mind as key ideas.

In read 4 Gareth was checking that his abstraction of the meaning of the sentence made sense. He paused at the end of unit 2 because he wanted to make sure that this phrase was the key to the whole sentence. He paused at the end of the sentence to try to put the main theme in his own words. In talking himself through his read record using the flow diagram as a guide, Gareth became much more aware of all the factors which influenced his strategy. For instance, he recognised that his previous knowledge about Darwin's theory of evolution and his particular purpose – abstracting the key idea – as well as the complex structure of the sentence and his own reading skills had influenced him. He explained that his strategy and tactics involved orienting to the general message, sampling for relevancy in relation to his purpose, selecting and reorganising the appropriate items from the sentence and finally checking his understanding. Gareth was beginning to reflect on his reading skills in *process* terms.

Summary

We have gone through this example rather slowly partly because it enabled us to recapitulate some earlier points (for example on tactics and read records) and partly because it gave us a chance to bring several things together and so give a better sense of the whole. It is probably better at this point to think through the example and make sure you have got it clear than to spend time practising. If, however, you would like an activity (that is, after all, one way of making sure that you understand the points being made) then you could try to work through an example for yourself. We shall be coming back to this in a later chapter and will then be working with passages of rather greater length. It is probably best, therefore, if you take a relatively short, fairly complex passage. If it is very short you may need to set it out one word per line, as in Fig. 5.1(b), so that your observer will be able to record your progress through the text. Set yourself a purpose, decide on a strategy, then read the passage. Afterwards, construct a flow diagram for the passage. Compare the diagram with the reading record produced by your observer and talk yourself through it as in the example. You should now be beginning to ask yourself the right questions, to think about the reading process in the more precise terms of the model we have presented. As always, it will help if you can discuss it with others; your observer, perhaps, or, if you are doing this in a group, with other members of the group. Remember, however, that the aim is to dispense with the help of others. They can be very helpful on the way, but in the end the conversation has to be with yourself.

6

Reading outcomes

Overview

In this chapter we shall be concerned with the results of our reading, the outcome of our engagement with the text. Often those results are easily identifiable and we are able to judge at once whether our reading has been successful. Most tests of reading outcome, such as the comprehension tests commonly used in school, work at this level. Sometimes, however, we are looking for a rather richer outcome from our reading, which such tests will not show. In this chapter we suggest a way of registering such a richer reading. Whatever our way of testing the outcome, however, the important thing is that by observing the results of our reading objectively we should be in a position to review the effectiveness of our approach.

Assessing reading outcomes – a traditional technique

Sometimes the outcome of our reading is straightforward and easy to identify. If, for example, our purpose in reading a certain paragraph were to find a particular fact then the outcome of our reading would be either that we had found the fact or that we had not. When the purpose is as specific and the outcome as easily identifiable as in this case it is fairly easy for us to judge the effectiveness of our reading. If the fact were indeed contained in the passage and we had missed it then the outcome was unsatisfactory and we should do something to improve the effectiveness of our reading.

Often, however, the issue is not as clear-cut. Our purpose may be not to find an easily identifiable fact but to grasp a rather complex theory; or we may need to go beyond just grasping the theory and to

76 *Reading to learn*

make judgements or inferences based upon it. In such cases the outcome of our reading will not be so easy to assess.

Yet it is important that we should make some effort to assess it, and to do so as objectively as we can, for it is the crucial test of the efficiency of our reading. If we pass it we can go forward fairly confident of the effectiveness of our strategies. If we fail we know there is something wrong.

But how do we go about developing our ability to assess outcome in these more difficult cases? The first step, as in the other chapters, is to find a way of externalising what goes on in our heads when we read. But, as in the other chapters, we have to remember that externalising is just an interim measure. We are bringing the process out into the daylight so that we can see its essential features and work on them. But at the end of the exercise the process has to return inside the head.

Now as it happens there is already a standard way of externalising reading outcomes in a form in which they can be tested: the traditional comprehension test. Typically (as in GCE O level) with such tests the reader is set a passage to read and then required to answer questions on it. Testing how far you have understood the test (the reading outcome) in this way has a number of advantages from an examiner's point of view. Above all, it can be fairly reliable in statistical terms. Comparisons between readers can be made relatively objectively. From our point of view, however, that of developing an individual's ability to read well, tests of this sort have severe defects. The chief one is that the monitoring of outcome is done from outside the individual. The questions are set and the answers marked by someone else. The checking of outcome is not part of the general process of self-monitoring with respect to reading that we have argued is necessary to genuine reading development. Unless the outcome is assessed by the reader himself or herself a vital part of the control system over reading is missing. For this reason we shall suggest later on an alternative to comprehension test-style assessment.

Comprehension tests do, however, have one important advantage. They are familiar to most readers. We shall, therefore, make use of them for our first activity, the purpose of which is to start you thinking about reading outcomes in more precise terms.

Reading outcomes 77

Activity 6.1   Checking on reading outcomes

First, *choose* a passage. It need not be very long. One about a page or half a page in length would do very well. Decide on a reading purpose. Now, before reading the passage if you can, *set yourself* one or more *questions* which, if you can answer them afterwards, will demonstrate that you have achieved the aim you set yourself in reading the passage. In some cases you may need to have a preliminary read before you will be able to set the questions. After you have set the questions, *read the passage through* making use of appropriate tactics and strategies. Now *write out answers* to your questions. Finally, by referring back to the passage, several times if necessary, check whether your answers seem right.

What you have done is, of course, to set yourself your own comprehension test. You may well have had difficulty first over setting good questions and then in being sure that you had marked your answers correctly. Do not worry about this. What the exercise has done is expose two things you can work on.

The first, setting good questions, is actually the more important. It is clearly related to work we did earlier, which will pay off now. We talked in Chapter 3 about formulating reading purposes in terms of questions, and emphasised the importance of being specific, especially about the level of comprehension aimed at.

Was one concerned only with identifying detail at the fairly literal level of comprehension? Was one identifying detail but doing something more, perhaps reorganising material into an abstract or summary? Or was one going beyond the material given in the text and making inferences about other applications or issues? Or are we operating on the material in a slightly different way, evaluating it or responding to it in terms of appreciation? The classification we offered then might be a helpful guide now:

5 Extrapolation
4 Evaluative
3 Appreciative
2 Reorganisational
1 Literal

78 *Reading to learn*

Our purpose is, of course, not classification but recognition of the level of comprehension aimed at, of the level of response the outcome should achieve. We noted earlier that certain 'command words' were often associated with particular levels of comprehension and that too might serve as a rough and ready help in framing questions.

Although the questions we set ourselves for testing our comprehension of a passage will be related to the questions we have arrived at through reformulating our reading purposes, they ought not to be the same. They ought to provide an independent check on whether the reading purpose was achieved.

We have suggested, at least as far as Activity 6.1 is concerned, that the check questions should be worked out at the same time as the reading purpose is formulated. Some people prefer to leave the check questions to a later stage. They can be worked out perfectly well after the whole reading has been carried out. The important thing is that they should be objective and specific and designed to test whether the purpose has indeed been achieved. Some people find it easier to make the shift to objectivity if they begin the checking operation with some such question to themselves as this: 'What would be a good question to test whether . . .?' etc. The temporary shift of role to that of examiner is made explicit (to oneself).

If you are doing this exercise in a group you may find it useful to work out your questions and then submit them to others for comment. Discussion often helps at this stage. In the end, however, it comes back to you. You have to decide whether your own questions are good enough.

Checking your own answers you will find, curiously, to be rather easier. If you have developed the habit of being honest with yourself about your reading you will find that, with practice, you soon develop a sense of whether your answers are on the right lines. Only initially will you want to go to the trouble of writing out your answers. It helps at the start because you need to stand a little away from your questions and answers and inspect and judge them. Writing out the answers helps you to be that little bit more objective. But the aim is to return the process into your head.

Assessing reading outcome in this way will help you to gain control over the way you read and to improve your effectiveness as a reader. There is, however, a danger in using comprehension-style techniques. They tend to encourage you to measure the outcome of your reading in terms of literal recall. There is a tendency to play safe and go for answers you can easily identify and easily measure. Now this may be perfectly all right in some cases. If, however, your purpose is a more complex one, if, for instance, you are seeking not just to understand the passage but to evaluate it, or if your intention is certainly to grasp the points made in the passage but then to go beyond them, to apply them in some other field, or to use them as a springboard from which to develop ideas of your own, then the kind of technique for assessing outcome that we have been discussing may be an unduly limiting one. There is a further danger. If you always assess the outcome of your reading in this kind of way then it may make the whole of your approach to reading rather rigid and mechanical. In the next section, therefore, we shall be putting forward a technique for assessing reading outcome which can accommodate richer outcomes. You certainly will not wish to use this technique all the time – it is too time-consuming – but you may find it appropriate on particular occasions. In any case, you may well wish to use it from time to time to, as it were, loosen up your reading. You may even use it deliberately to promote a more creative mode of reading as a permanent part of your reading repertoire.

Registering a richer reading outcome

The technique, developed at the Centre for the Study of Human Learning, is known as the 'structures of meaning' technique. Basically it is a way of registering the various ideas that come into your mind when you are reading and using them to test the quality of your response to the passage. Exhibiting the relationships between the ideas brings home to you connections which you yourself have made while reading the passage, connections which may not, speaking in purely literal terms, have been 'in' the passage itself. It then becomes possible to compare the 'structure of meaning' which you have created with, say, the structure of the text as exhibited in a flow diagram.

A step-by-step account of the 'structures of meaning' technique

STEP ONE. ELICITING THE IDEAS

1 Start by going over the reading event in your head. Try to

80 *Reading to learn*

become more aware of the thoughts and feelings which were triggered off by the text.

2 On separate sheets of paper write down every idea you can think of and number each sheet to record the order. Each idea represents one item of meaning.

3 If the ideas flow easily proceed until some twenty or thirty are recorded.

4 If the flow dries up try some of the following tricks:

Examine the preceding sheets one by one and try to relive the reading experience which prompted you to respond in terms of the item on each sheet.

Think of your purposes for reading the text and of how you responded to them as you read.
Work on one item and imagine vivid visual portrayals of it. Push yourself to think of alternatives.
Think of the item in a new context or imagine some bizarre associations.
Try interrogating yourself about the text and your purposes for reading it.

Accept the free flow of ideas and keep recording these on separate bits of paper.

STEP TWO. RELATING THE ITEMS

By asking 'what goes with what?' various patterns emerge.

1 Start by looking at each item quickly and in succession to get an overview. This will help you to establish a preliminary basis for sorting.

2 Now go through sorting the items into separate piles.

3 As you proceed, be prepared to change your mind and reallocate the items.

4 At the end examine the piles and decide to re-sort, split up or amalgamate the piles.

5 Ask yourself if the piles sort into distinctive categories. Do not define these at this stage.

6 Examine the items in each pile and lay these out visually in some spatial relationship which exhibits their meaning (see the next step).

Figure 6.1 Diagrammatic illustration of a meaning net

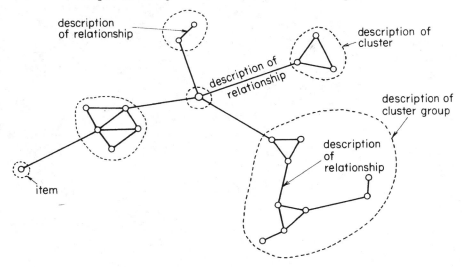

STEP THREE. DISPLAYING THE PATTERN

One useful way of displaying the pattern is in the form of a network. What such a form will show is the way in which ideas cluster into distinct patterns of meaning.

1 Look in turn at the cluster of items constituting each pile and say what the items have in common. We can call this a cluster description.
2 Consider each cluster description and lay out the clusters in a way which expresses the relationships between them. (For example, two clusters might depend in some way on another one, one of the two (but not the other) might lead on to some other cluster, and so on.)
3 Look at the relationships between the clusters and try to describe what the relationship is.

Fig. 6.1 shows what the net could look like in some circumstances.

The 'structures of meaning' technique produces two things: first, ideas which though in a sense a product of the text are not themselves contained within the text, and, secondly, patterns of meaning which though derived from the text cut across the pattern given by the text. It indicates, therefore, the extent to which the

82 *Reading to learn*

reader has been stimulated to produce additional ideas and to perceive new relationships between and implications of ideas. Implicit in the approach is a conception of the text not as repository but as springboard. Now you may not always want to treat the text in this way, but what the technique exhibits is as genuinely a reading outcome as the 'answers' written out to your comprehension-style questions.

Fig. 6.2 sets out the technique in tabular form.

Figure 6.2 How to display a reading outcome in structured form

Step 1 Eliciting items of meaning
The number of items can be from about 4 to 50 or more. Obviously this depends on the length of text and on your experience of it. To begin with do not use more than 20–30 items

Step 2 Sorting and defining the relationships between items
By asking 'what goes with what?' the items gradually become sorted

Step 3 Constructing the pattern
By asking 'in what way are the items related?' a pattern emerges

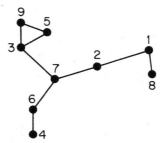

Reading outcomes 83

Activity 6.2 **Showing reading outcome in 'structure of meaning' form**

Choose a text which you are likely to read in the context of your normal reading to learn activity. Specify your reading purposes. Read the text. Draw up a 'structure of meaning' to display your understanding of the text.

Using a meaning net to assess reading outcome

Now of course all that we have done so far is to put forward a new way of externalising your reading outcome. What we still have to do is to use the new technique to assess our reading. One way of doing that might be to look at the number of ideas produced by the technique and say: 'Heavens! That looks a lot!' and go on to assess the outcome as good. Or we might note a number of relationships which we had not perceived before and conclude that the outcome was pretty satisfactory. Certainly if no new ideas are produced and not many new relationships or implications perceived then the outcome can be deemed a relatively unproductive one. But then number may not be the important thing. Suppose you produced just one extra idea and that was a very important one? Or suppose you saw how just one set of relationships could be re-expressed but that was a crucial step in the development of your understanding of the field – what then?

The point that needs to be emphasised is that the purpose of assessing outcome is to check on the efficacy of the procedures we have adopted to read the passage. Our concern is with process not content. For this reason we would prefer to use the 'structures of meaning' technique to review systematically all the phases of the reading to learn approach. This is the best way in which we can use our externalisation of reading outcome. The procedure for doing that is set out below. We have set it out in some detail to give you an idea of the kinds of questions you can ask yourself. Normally you would pick and choose among items, selecting according to their appropriateness to your particular circumstances. Again, you will certainly not wish to use this procedure regularly. It is best seen as something which you should do from time to time to give added reinforcement to your command over your reading techniques.

84   *Reading to learn*

Using a meaning net for review

Ask yourself:
How many of the ideas elicited in your net can actually be traced back to the text?
What does this reveal about the kinds of comprehension you made?
How selective were you? Did you miss important things?
If unselective, did you succeed in achieving an accurate verbatim report of the text?
Did you modify the text by
- paraphrase
- reorganisation
- inference?
How evaluative was your comprehension?

More specifically on strategy: in terms of your purpose and your knowledge of the text were you
too obsessed with detail
too selective
too evaluative or not evaluative enough
too inferential or not inferential enough
over- or under-elaborate in your tactics and overall strategy?
When you were constructing your meaning net
what order did the items appear in? Were they apparently random? Was there some pattern?
What does this tell you about the way in which you reconstructed the outcome of your reading?
More generally on the outcome as shown in the meaning net:
What is your current understanding of the passage?
How does this differ from that expressed in your meaning net?
Add, delete or rearrange items and clusters to show your present understanding.
Was your meaning net more or less adequate?
Now, more systematically, review the whole reading process, taking into account the information provided by the meaning net.
Review purpose. (Was it specific enough, were there sub-purposes you should have formulated?)
Review strategy. (Were the tactics the right ones?)
Review outcome.

Reading outcomes 85

It may be helpful to take an actual case as an example. Figs. 6.3 and 6.4 were both produced by a student named Lisa. Fig. 6.3 shows her meaning net as it originally was before review. Fig. 6.4 shows the meaning net after review.

As can be seen, Lisa's net after review shows a number of additional items, ideas which she had added after looking back at the text in the course of her review, two additional clusters, and a revised sketch of the relationships between clusters.

What this suggested to Lisa was that she had missed quite a lot of what was in the passage. Her original meaning net reflected her understanding of the passage all right, but when she came to review it by comparing it with the passage she found that it was deficient. The outcome was not completely satisfactory. Thinking over the possible reasons for this, she felt fairly happy about the way she had formulated her reading purpose but much less happy about her reading strategy, which she felt had been too slapdash. She had employed one quick 'smooth' read followed by a fairly uncontrolled 'item' read. She decided on review that her purpose, which was of a fairly high order in terms of comprehension demanded (it was 'evaluative'), would have been better served if she had employed a 'search' read and a more rigorous 'item' read.

Figure 6.3   Lisa's meaning net before review

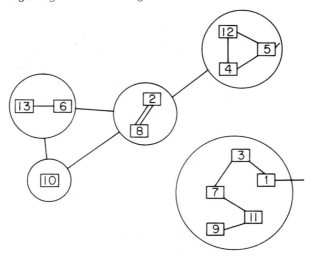

86   *Reading to learn*

Figure 6.4   Lisa's meaning net after review

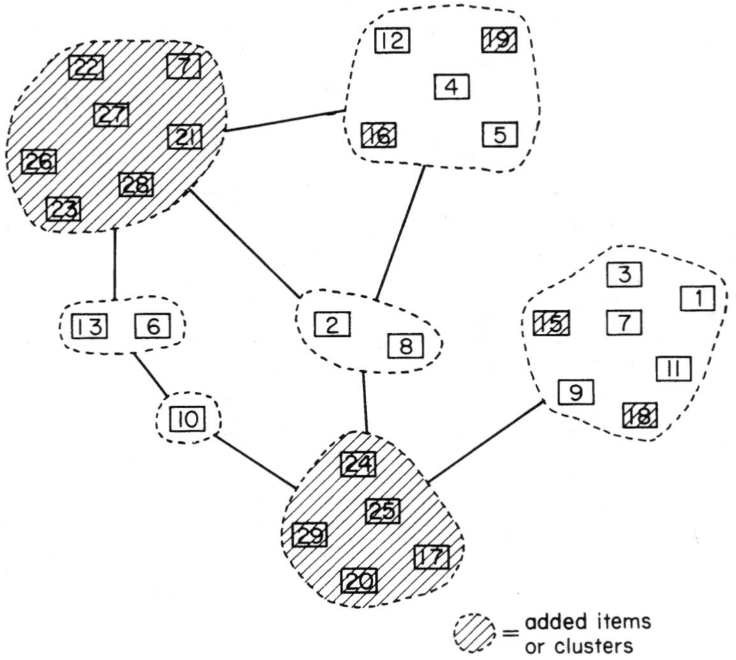

= added items
or clusters

Activity 6.3   **Using a meaning net to review outcome**

Choose a passage. Formulate a purpose. Read the passage. Elicit a 'structure of meaning'. Display it in the form of a meaning net (you could use the material you produced for Activity 6.2 if you wished). Use the meaning net, together with the text, to review the outcome of your read.

Summary

Whatever means you employ to identify outcome the important thing is that you should make some effort to assess the results of your reading. Only if you check outcome are you likely to face realistically the issue of the effectiveness of your tactics and strategy.

7
Becoming a competent reader: putting it together

Overview

In Chapter 1 we outlined our model of the reading to learn process. The four key concepts in that model were purpose, strategy, outcome and review, and we explored each of these in turn in the chapters which followed. Our aim was to show how the reader could increase control over his reading by concentrating on these four elements in his reading process. Inevitably, in discussing one we had to talk about others. Our whole argument is that reading to learn is a subtle, complex, dynamic thing. The different parts of the process interact. We have separated the parts out in order to focus on them better. Now, however, we need to put them together again. In this chapter we look at the reading to learn process as a whole, by bringing all the parts together in one major activity. We then go on to sketch how the reader can plan a reading development programme for him or her self.

The reading process seen as a whole

In Chapter 3 we saw that reading is influenced by a reader's purpose. What a reader seeks to get from reading a passage affects the way he or she approaches the passage, the extent to which one part of the text rather than another is concentrated on, the different kind of attention which various parts of the text receive. Purpose, we saw, governs the reader's initial choice of tactics. But this is not a once and for all matter. The reader may decide that a certain part of the text should receive detailed reading and so he assigns it an item read. However, as he gets into the text he may conclude that

88 *Reading to learn*

that particular part of it is less relevant than he thought, and so may switch to a smooth read, skimming through the text more rapidly. While reading another part of the passage he might suddenly realise, perhaps when nearing the end of that section, that this was more relevant than he had initially thought, and so might re-read the section with a sharper eye to what he wanted (search read).

This kind of flexible, semi-subconscious self-monitoring is going on all the time with an aware reader, and it leads to a constant revision of the elements in a reader's approach as he proceeds. In the example above he decided to change tactics and strategy. But it could also be that as he read he realised that there was more to the passage than he had thought, and that he had formulated his original reading purpose in far too narrow terms. He might, therefore, at this stage revise his reading purpose, and this, in turn, might affect the relative importance of different parts of the text, and hence the tactics he had adopted for dealing with them.

When the reading process is considered as a whole it turns out to be a highly dynamic business. Each of the components could be worked on separately. What we must do now is take more fully into account their interdependence.

Let us first recapitulate what we should be aiming at. When reading a passage to learn something from it we should:

1 define our reading purposes adequately
2 choose and use reading tactics and strategies appropriately
3 check our reading outcome against purpose and text
4 review our effectiveness by appraising 1–3 both separately and together.

Let us now apply these precepts to a major piece of reading in Activity 7.1. Throughout this book we have tried to relate activities to the reading to learn that you are actually doing, believing not only that in this way the whole exercise would become more real for you, but also that reading purposes etc. should arise genuinely from the reader's knowledge, needs and context. We have, therefore, usually suggested that you choose an appropriate text yourself. On this occasion we are supplying the text so that we can better control the supporting material. However, we think you will find the text both interesting and relevant. It is not, of course, genuinely part of your normal reading and so for this once, admittedly artificially, we

Becoming a competent reader: putting it together 89

have suggested some reading purposes. The text, 'Students' use and misuse of reading skills', is part of an address given some years ago by W. G. Perry at Harvard University.

The aim of this activity is to increase your awareness of the reading to learn process as a whole. The activity provides an opportunity to revise your knowledge of the separate components which make up your reading to learn model but the principal intention is to focus attention on the way they work together. This activity is an extended one and you might need to devote as much as an hour to it.

Activity 7.1   **Reading to learn: the process as a whole**

Preliminary

On this occasion, because we are supplying the text, you should begin by skimming the article to get an overview of its contents and be aware of what you are doing. Do this very quickly. Don't spend more than 2–3 minutes on it. Scan the paragraphs, sampling beginnings and endings. Do not read all the sentences.
Now,

1 Choose a purpose from those we give on pages 97–8.
2 Reflect on the purpose, formulating it as a question if you wish, but certainly trying to make it as specific as you can. Try to be clear about the level and nature of comprehension involved (Chapter 3).
3 Write a plan of how you intend to read the article to achieve the purpose(s) you have specified: the reading tactics and overall strategy which you will employ (Chapter 2).
4 Note the time you begin to read the article and the time you finish it.
5 Record your strategy. For present purposes the simple self-recording technique using pencil tracking in the margin will be sufficient (see Chapter 2, page 22. Remember to record all reads. You may use the other techniques described earlier if you wish, but for those you will need an observer.
6 Read the article.

90 *Reading to learn*

Students' use and misuse of reading skills

W. G. Perry

1 Mr President, twenty years ago this Faculty undertook an experiment to see if some of its students could be taught to read better. Since the Faculty was then something of a pioneer in such an enterprise, it would seem appropriate that it should receive, after two decades, at least a report of progress – the more so because the work now concerns not the correction of the disabilities of a few students but the direction of the abilities of a large proportion of the freshman class.

2 The students of this college are reputed to spend a good deal of time reading. In fact, a student sits with his books for nearly a thousand hours each year. The Faculty has a deep concern that these hours be fruitful. This concern is evident in the wording of assignments, in the layout of instruction in each course, and in the conversations of teachers with their students. It was this same concern that started the original experiment in reading improvement in 1938. The experiment began with a rather mechanical emphasis. It consisted of an instructor whose main job was to run a projector for the first Harvard Reading Films, and of some thirty student volunteers, hopefully the worst readers in the freshman class (and at that time there apparently were some freshmen who for Harvard's intents and purposes found it hard to read at all). The class met for about 18 to 20 sessions and engendered enough enthusiasm to become, like many an experiment, a kind of annual fixture, this one known as the Remedial Reading Course. Each year freshmen as they arrived in the fall would take a reading test and those who scored lowest would be informed of their plight and allowed to volunteer for the continued experiment.

3 When the Bureau of Study Counsel took over the actual instruction in this course in 1946, we met with thirty depressed-looking volunteers one evening in a basement classroom somewhere. Not knowing really what we were up against, we gave still another reading test of a standard sort and discovered that every single one of them could score better on this test than 85% of the college freshmen in the country. We felt that to be useful to these people in their genuine dissatisfaction we were going to have to take a new look at the reading improvement

Becoming a competent reader: putting it together 91

game. We therefore abandoned the word '*Remedial*' for the course and upgraded the material until it could jar the teeth of the average graduate student. Then we threw the doors open.

4 The amount of enthusiasm that exists in this community to read better – or if not better, then at least faster – is evidenced by the fact that we soon found ourselves with nearly 800 people enrolled in the course. When we examined the roll, we found that we had some 400 freshmen from Harvard and Radcliffe, 150 upperclassmen, 230 graduate students from the various schools, especially that of Business Administration, and 2 professors – from the Law School.

5 Although the fees paid by these multitudes looked very attractive on the budget of a small office, we came to feel this was stretching our energies too far. We have subsequently cut the class in half and have been trying to make some sensible system of priorities whereby we might offer first chance on seats to roughly that third of the freshmen class that might be most likely to benefit from this kind of instruction. In trying to find out who these people might be, we have turned up some observations about freshmen, which may be of interest to the Faculty.

6 One wonders first of all why students who read, on tests, as well as these do, should want to attend a reading course at all, much less one that meets daily at 8 o'clock in the morning. Of course a number come in hope of magic – some machine they've heard of that will stretch their eyes until they can see a whole page at a glance. This is understandable. Freshmen are deprived rather abruptly of the luxury of thinking that reading is something they can finish, and are confronted instead with an infinite world of books in which they sense that they may forever feel behind, or even illiterate.

7 But year by year it has become more apparent that what the students lack is not mechanical skills but flexibility and purpose in the use of them – the capacity to adjust themselves to the variety of reading materials and purposes that exist on a college level.

8 What they seem to do with almost any kind of reading is to open the book and read from word to word, having in advance abandoned all responsibility in regard to the purpose of the reading to those who had made the assignment. They complain

92 *Reading to learn*

consequently of difficulty in concentrating and feel that they have 'read' whole assignments but are unable to remember anything in them. We have therefore shifted the emphasis of the reading course away from mechanics over to an effort to shake students loose from this conscientious but meaningless approach to their work. We have found that if they can be persuaded of their right to think, even though reading, they can then develop a broader and more flexible attack on the different forms of study and put their skills to meaningful use even on long assignments.

9   In offering freshmen priority on seats on the course, therefore, we have naturally wanted to know about their flexibility and their sense of purpose in reading. This is a hard thing to measure. To make some estimate of it we designed a new kind of reading test – as reading tests go it may really be rather peculiar – and presented it to the freshmen of Harvard and Radcliffe when they arrived this September. We suspected the students might learn more from it than we would, but this seemed a legitimate chance to take. I should like to describe this test and to tell you what the students did with it.

10 First of all, instead of the usual short passages which appear on reading tests, we presented students with thirty pages of detailed material – a complete chapter from a history book. We asked them to imagine that they were enrolled in a course entitled The Growth of Western Institutions. We asked them to picture themselves sitting down of an evening to study one assignment in this course – the chapter entitled 'The Development of the English State, 1066–1272'. They were to suppose that they had two hours ahead of them for this work, but that after all, they still had their French to do and some Chemistry to review before they went to bed. At the same time, they were to imagine that in this course an hour-examination would be given in about a week on which they would be asked to write a short essay and to '*identify*' important details. We told them that this was a test of what they derived from the early stages of their study of regular assignments and that in about 20 minutes or so we would stop them and ask them questions appropriate to their particular method of work. We then turned them loose.

11 Twenty-two minutes later we stopped them and asked them what they had been doing. If they reported that they had been

Becoming a competent reader: putting it together 93

reading from the very beginning and going straight ahead into the chapter – whether rapidly the first reading, or carefully with a more rapid view in mind – we gave them a regular multiple choice question on the chapter as far as they had gone in it. Up to this point the test was fairly standard, and we can report that the vast majority of the students, over 90% of them in fact, reported that this was exactly what they had done. We can report that their rate of work in this particular approach was astonishing and their capacity to answer multiple-choice questions on detail was impressive. Some of them had read as many as twenty pages of very detailed material and were able to answer accurately every sensible question we could ask them, about the detail.

12 The freshman class – as far as we could see – of both Harvard and Radcliffe, consisted of a most remarkable collection of readers – in the narrow sense of the term. The showing is most remarkable because, of course, these 90% of the class were going at this chapter in the hardest way imaginable.

13 Let me explain what I mean. The chapter in question is an admirable piece of exposition, but like many admirable chapters it makes no initial statement of its aims, and it takes a little while to get going, and as a consequence, the reader who begins at the beginning with the Battle of Hastings and reads word by word is likely to find himself at page three hopelessly bogged down in the shires, the hundreds and the marches of Anglo-Saxon England. And after ten minutes or so, this was just where the students reported themselves to be. What we were interested to determine was how many students in the face of this burden of detail, the purpose of which was not clear, would have the moral courage – or should we call it the immoral courage – to pull themselves out and look at the ending of the chapter. Or even to survey the entire marginal gloss set out like sign posts page by page. The very ending has a bold flag out beside it which says – '*Recapitulation*'. As a summary paragraph we doubt that we have ever seen a better one. From a half minute of study of this paragraph the whole development of the chapter becomes immediately clear to the reader and puts him in a strong position, not only to select among details as he reads them, but also to remember, for their meaningfulness, the details he would need to support an intelligent discourse.

94 *Reading to learn*

14 Out of these 1500 of the finest freshman readers in the country only one hundred and fifty even made a claim to have taken a look ahead during twenty minutes of struggle with the chapter. And the vast majority of these seemed to have looked ahead only to determine how long the assignment was.

15 We asked anyone who could do so to write a short statement about what the chapter was all about. The number who were able to tell us in terms that had something to do with the growth of institutions, was just one in a hundred-fifteen.

16 As a demonstration of obedient purposelessness in the reading of 99% of freshmen we found this impressive. We had been looking for the one-third of the class most in need of our beneficient instruction and we had found just about everybody. We tried to find out if the students had behaved this way simply because it was a test – they reported no, that they always worked this way. When we pointed the ending to them, some said, '*You mean you can sometimes tell what a chapter is about by looking at the end*', and others said, '*Oh Lord, how many times have I been told*'.

17 Told or not, after twelve years of reading home-work assignments in school they had all settled into the habit of leaving the point of it all to someone else. We knew from our own efforts to teach independence of approach in reading that students find it hard to hear us even when the sheer bulk of college work could be handled in no other way. And we supposed that school teachers had an even harder time of it. We were therefore prepared to find this widespread passivity of purpose; we wished to go beyond this and to identify those students whose misconceptions of reading involved something worse, a positive misconception of aim, a notion of the purpose of reading so at variance with the goals of Harvard that they might be especially slow at learning from their college experience. We had therefore added another turn to our test.

18 We asked the students to imagine further that in their imaginary course an examination had been given on which an essay question on this chapter had appeared. The question (which we hoped was a proper type Harvard essay question) read: '*From 1066–1272, the Norman and Angevin kings laid the foundations of English self-government both by their strengths and by their weaknesses*'. – Discuss. (Twenty minutes.) We then presented

Becoming a competent reader: putting it together 95

them with two answers, purporting to have been written by two students. The first of these was a chronological reiteration of the chapter by a student with an extraordinary memory for dates and kings and no concern for the question (or for any intellectual issue at all, for that matter). We calculated that no instructor with a shred of compassion in him could give this answer less than a C – even though it might deserve less. The second essay answer, shorter, and with hardly a date in it, addressed itself stringently to the issues posed by the question. We supposed this answer to be worth a B +, or perhaps an A – to a relieved instructor.

19 In validating the test, we had then begged the assistance of the chief section man in a real course, not wholly unlike this imaginary course of ours, and asked him to grade the essays. On the first, he said that he really couldn't give the student a D because he had worked so hard; of the second we were pleased to hear him say that this was obviously an A student, even though all he was going to get on this essay was a B +.

20 To the freshmen, then, we presented on the test these two answers without reporting their value and asked them to state which of the essays was the better, which the worse, and to given their reasons. We are happy to say that on this they did quite well. Only two hundred students graded the better essay the worse, and only two hundred more gave the wrong reasons for the correct grading. This means that, on this particular measure, only a rough third of our freshmen showed themselves to be headed toward the wrong goals. Very possibly, were this same test to be given later in the year, the percentage would be less. But we have experience to support that the tendency persists – often tragically.

21 These were then the students to whom we turned our attention. Until such students revise their sense of the purpose of reading, an increase in effort is likely to produce only worse results. Oddly, we have as yet found nothing else to distinguish them from other people. The number of them who come from public schools as against private schools is exactly the same as for the class as a whole, and they are by no means the least intelligent members of their class. We are eager to find if we can learn more about how they get their misconceptions. We hope that the Reading Course may help to turn some of them around.

96   *Reading to learn*

Perhaps the test itself helped; the section man who helped us with the test was quick to point out its instructional possibilities, and we gave the text and essays to the students to take with them, together with a page of comments. It was encouraging to have to thread one's way afterwards through knots of students working over their papers.

22   What might the faculty conclude from all this. As the faculty's agent in this area, I can report my own conclusions from this twenty-year experiment.

1   It appears that most students can learn to read better.

2   The instruction that assists them to do so does not centre in the mechanics of reading. The mechanics of reading skill are inseparable at this level from the individual's purpose as he reads. If you train someone in mechanics alone, he drops right back into his old habits the minute he picks up an assigned test.

3   The possession of excellent reading skills as evidenced on conventional reading tests is no guarantee that a student knows how to read long assignments meaningfully. The fact that the Admissions Committee is providing students of higher and higher ability should not lull the Faculty into feeling that at last it does not have to teach students how to study. In fact the responsibility is only the greater, for these students have the ability to muddle through assignments the wrong way and still get that wretched C −.

4   There can be no general rules for teaching the exercise of judgement in reading. Such judgement requires courage, and courage cannot be taught by rule, it can only be dared, or redirected, in ways appropriate to particular subjects and learning tasks. To be sure, the reading of conflicting authorities is a fertile ground for young courage, and an excellent exercise in reading skill. And a C − for the attainment of useless knowledge is perhaps less of a kindness in the long run than congratulations for effort and a clean E for expending it in the wrong game. However, the individual instructor in his own course remains the best judge of how to set up his assignments so that they demand a redirection of effort toward judgement and away from ritual.

5   A short separate course of general instruction, like the Reading Class, can be of some contributing value, if only

Becoming a competent reader: putting it together 97

because it offers a moment's freedom to experiment without the threat of failure. But its limits are very clear. In such a course we can only dramatise the issues, and this only in the area of very general expository reading. We can refer only briefly to science and must leave literature explicitly alone. We feel, too, that only a narrow line of spirit divides such instruction from an invitation to mere gamesmanship. We sometimes worry, in teaching method without content, lest students gather that we recommend a glance reading at the ending of chapters and at nothing else. (We do dare students to suppose that even this is sometimes appropriate.)

23 I should like to be able to report, in conclusion, that when we do succeed in introducing students to the rigors of thoughtful reading they are invariably grateful. I must confess, a bit ruefully, that this is not always the case. I have here a description of this kind of instruction in a student's words. To assist us in developing the course we have occasionally given the students a questionnaire at the end, and this one of a year or so ago was a real up-to-date Social Science type questionnaire: open ended at the beginning, pointed at the end, and all. It says here, '*What did you expect when you came to this course?*' Big space. '*What do you think about it now?*' Big space. On the other side a lot of specific questions. We did not ask students to sign their names, only to enter the scores they made at the beginning and end of the course.

24 This student's scores when he came to the Course showed him to have derived only a D − kind of understanding from considerable study of the material. At the end he was obtaining a straight A understanding in one third of the time. I remember settling back with this one in anticipation of those comments that a teacher so loves to hear − but not at all. He was furious. '*What did you expect when you came to this course?*' '*I expected an organised effort to improve my reading.*' '*What do you think about it now?*' '*This has been the sloppiest and most disorganised course I have ever taken. Of course, I have made some progress, but this was due entirely to my own efforts . .*'

Suggested reading purposes for this article

1 Read to select and recall, say, seven specific bits of information

98 *Reading to learn*

(details such as numbers, dates, events, arguments). Link these units of information together within a general theme, e.g. a reading test, criteria for selecting volunteers, a Harvard Reading Course.

2 Read to summarise the central message of the text. This summary should be clearly understandable by a non-specialist in the field.

3 Read to draw inferences from key issues in the text. Try to relate the main ideas to your own experiences and interests and attempt to go creatively beyond the author's ideas.

4 Read to evaluate the article. Does the author achieve his purpose? You should consider strength or weakness of argument, the author's selection of facts, choice of words, style etc.

5 Invent your own purpose and specify as above (e.g. to check for Americanisms – spelling, terms, choice of words, concepts and values).

The purposes given above are all cognitive. You might like to try an effective purpose (e.g. to fantasise about the student's life).

You have formulated your reading purpose; you have chosen your reading tactics; and you have used them in reading the passage. The next step is to *check your outcome*, which we do first against purpose and then against text.

Checking outcome against purpose

First, establish the outcome of your read. For the purposes of this exercise write it out in some detail. Put comprehension-style questions to yourself and write down your answer.

Next, read the four pieces which follow. Each is actually an outcome written out by a student after he had read the Perry text. Which outcome most matches yours?

Piece 1

Twenty years ago an experiment was undertaken because students spend nearly 1000 hours reading each year. The original experiment started in 1938 with the concern that these hours should be fruitful.

Thirty student volunteers came for 18 to 20 sessions and generated enough enthusiasm for the experiment to become an

Becoming a competent reader: putting it together 99

annual feature. When the course was taken over in 1946, the thirty volunteers were given another reading test and scored better than 85% of college freshmen. The course was then upgraded and opened to anyone. Nearly 800 enrolled and the staff were forced to reduce this number to one-third. In the process some interesting observations from a new reading test were made. This test was 30 pages of detailed historical material about 'The Development of the English State, 1066–1272'. The students were told to imagine they had two hours to study this but would be stopped after 20 minutes. They were asked what they were doing and given a multiple choice test. Ninety per cent started at the beginning and did well on the question on detail.

Out of 1500 only 150 claimed to look ahead. Only one in a hundred (i.e. 15) could say what the chapter was about.

In another test the students had to imagine they were set a 20-minute exam question. They were then presented with two answers: one factual and worth C −, the other essay was shorter and addressed itself to the question and was worth an A −. Two hundred students gave the better essay as the worse, and 200 gave the wrong reasons for the correct grading. Roughly one-third of the students were heading for the wrong goals.

Students can learn to read better, although one student who obtained D − at the beginning and A at the end in one-third of the time, thought the course was sloppy and badly organised.

Piece 2

Some time ago the Faculty decided to undertake an experiment to see if students could be taught to read better. Students spend a lot of time reading and the Faculty was concerned that this time should be fruitful.

The original course had a mechanical emphasis but generated enough enthusiasm to become a regular annual feature. Later volunteers were found to score high on a conventional reading test, so the course material was upgraded and the course opened to anyone.

Students do not lack mechanical skills but the flexibility and purpose in their use of them. The course emphasis was, therefore, to shake them from their conscientious but meaningless approach to their work. A new type of test was developed that showed most of

100 *Reading to learn*

the class were going about a reading task in the hardest possible way; they were unable to pull themselves away from the detail, they demonstrated obedient purposelessness. A second test was to identify those students whose misconceptions involved a positive misconception of purpose. Because, until those students who value factual detail revise their sense of purpose, an increase in effort for them is likely to produce only worse results.

The important conclusion was that students could learn to read better. But they are not always grateful when introduced to the rigours of thoughtful reading.

Piece 3

The author gives a very interesting but superficial account of an experiment continued over many years to see if some of the students could be taught to read better. This was considered worthwhile as the students spend many hours reading and there was a general concern that this time should be spent fruitfully. He presents figures of how many students are inflexible readers. These figures are the numbers of students who did not look to the end of the chapter during a 20-minute study period, were able to answer detailed multiple choice questions, but were not able to give an account of what the chapter was about. The author includes in these numbers students who were reading 'rapidly or carefully with a more rapid read in mind'. The students may have assumed or preferred to abstract out the important details *after* they had done an initial detailed read. Therefore this test does not aid the author's point that the students are inflexible, because there is no evidence that they could not operate in other ways for other tasks, or that they may have shown more varied approaches after their first read. It does show that when given this test situation they tend to opt for factual learning initially.

The second test also supports this criticism. Most of the students (two-thirds) selected the best essay and probably could have written such an essay if they were given sufficient study time. The other third may be on the wrong lines only in so far as they assume that this is what the college values, but may not value this themselves.

The author goes on to say that he *hoped* that the reading course helps to turn some of these students around, and that perhaps the test helped in this. He gives as evidence that the students were seen

Becoming a competent reader: putting it together 101

working on the essays after the class was dismissed. Has he not got better evidence as to the effectiveness of the course than this?

Very few of his conclusions are substantiated by the material that precedes them. He gives no evidence that students can be taught to read better, nor does he give any details of the reading course and of how he teaches them to read better after they have done the initial tests.

Piece 4

This article suggests that many students have not learnt to formulate their own purposes for reading or to apply flexible reading skills to achieve these purposes. This is assumed to be a limitation of the students.

These students, however, have been admitted to Harvard, one of America's top universities, and are presumably of the best qualified students in the country. This suggests that far from gaining C−s, they have been achieving top grades in their schools. Their performance has probably been optimally adapted to the goal of getting to Harvard and to the criteria that has been operating in their schools. Thus the criticism should be directed to the school system rather than the students. The schools are over prescriptive and do not allow for individuality of purpose that opportunities for formulating one's own purpose would require. Also, because of the sophistication required to prescribe and evaluate a 'higher level' learning task, the schools and exam system have emphasised factual learning.

Therefore this article although very reasonable in its approach to changing the values of the successes of the educational system, does not expose the culprits − namely the schools and exams. If Harvard really does value non-factual learning, perhaps it should select its students differently and campaign for a re-direction of the schools.

In fact, each student had chosen a different purpose from among the ones listed earlier. The outcomes relate, therefore, to different purposes.

Which purpose goes with which piece? (The answers are given at the end of the chapter.)

Was the outcome which you chose as most nearly matching yours inspired by the same purpose as yours?

The chances are that it will have been (if that is not the case then

102 *Reading to learn*

you need to do more work on purpose specification and should read the next paragraph or so with extra attention). This should bring home to you the extent to which purpose influences outcome. To consolidate that point you should, however, reflect briefly on the relationship in each case. Try to describe each piece and how it matches or differs from your own. If you think that your outcome did not really match any of the four pieces that may not matter. Consider how it differed from them and ask yourself whether the differences are significant. Finally, examine to what extent your outcome satisfies the purpose you originally set yourself.

Checking outcome against text

For this part of the activity you will need a flow diagram for the text. Normally you would draw up your own (Chapters 4 and 5). Again in the interests of control, however, we are supplying a flow diagram for you (Fig. 7.1). The flow diagram describes all twenty-four paragraphs as they relate to each other according to (a) order in the text (the vertical columns) (b) categories of description, i.e. text link, main theme, qualifications, elaboration (horizontal columns). You will also need your: purpose; outcome; read record; description of strategy.

Go through the flow diagram and mark (preferably in colour) those paragraphs most relevant to your purpose. When you have finished, stand back. Look at the pattern revealed. This should at once tell you something about the type of selectivity (if any!) which you should have been exercising while reading. If you now look at your read record you should be able to tell whether you did exercise it.

Your written outcome will provide another check. Compare it with your marked flow diagram, which highlights relevance in terms of your chosen purpose, and ask yourself:

Did I miss important details?
Did I include too much detail?
Were there parts of the passage I should have concentrated on more?
Were there parts which were less important than I had supposed?

Your answers will have implications for your review of strategy, to which you should now turn.

Becoming a competent reader: putting it together 103

Figure 7.1 Students' use and misuse of reading skills

Para	Text link	Main theme	Qualification	Elaboration
1	Reading course progress report justified: a b			
2		Students spend much time reading. Faculty concerned that this fruitful. Those who score lowest in conventional reading test allowed to volunteer on the course.		
3		To be useful, reading course was ungraded and doors opened.		
4				800 enrolled
5		Sensible system of priorities needed to select multitudes. In developing priority, interesting observations made about students.		
6	One wonders why so many freshmen come – feel behind, feel illiterate, exposed to so many books – hope for magic.			
7		Students lack not mechanical skills, but flexibility and purpose in use of skills.		
8			Students abandon responsibility as regards purpose.	
9		Priority determined by 2 criteria: flexibility and purpose. New test devised.		
10			Details of test.	
11			Results of test: – most students read from beg. to end – " " successful in objective tests.	
12		Most of class read chapter in hardest possible way.		
13			Students bogged down in welter of detail.	
14				Only 150/1,500 looked ahead.
15				Only 1/115 could tell what text was about.
16		Most freshmen demonstrate obedient purposelessness.		
17		Need to go beyond this to identify positive misconception of purpose.		
18			Details of test	
19			Validation of test	
20			Results of test – 1/3 students heading wrong goals.	
21		This 1/3 student population was given priority on the course.		
22		CONCLUSION		
23	Students grateful.			
24	Some exceptions.			

Reviewing strategy and tactics

Review the way you read the text, jogging your memory by using the pencil record you made in the margin. Start at the beginning of the pencil track and move slowly along it with your finger. Try to remember, with the aid of the markings and by referring to the text,

104   *Reading to learn*

what you were doing at particular points. Do this for each of your reads.

Talk yourself through. You may find it helpful to refer back to Chapter 2 where we give example of the kinds of questions you should be asking, of the sort of conversation you should be having with yourself.

At the end *stand back* from the reconstruction of your read and ask yourself about your strategy generally:

Did you keep to the strategy you outlined in your original plan?
Judging by reference to outcome, was it broadly right?
Was the combination of tactics effective?
Were the tactics used in the right order?
Did you carry out the tactics effectively?
If you were to do it all again, would you use the same combination of tactics or would you plan another strategy?
Was the strategy the right one to achieve your purpose?
How satisfied are you with the outcome of your read?

Inevitably in reviewing strategy you find yourself referring to outcome, and in checking outcome you find yourself referring to strategy. The order in which you conduct your review can vary. You may prefer to talk yourself through your read immediately after finishing the read and while it is still fresh in your mind, and leave checking outcome till later. Whatever you do you will find that you need to be referring continually from one component to another. Purpose, strategy and outcome are inter-related and in reviewing one you will find yourself reviewing others. They all influence each other.

Reviewing purpose–strategy–outcome together

At the end of your review stand back from the whole process and just think out the connections between the parts:

Was your purpose specific enough?
Was your strategy the right one to achieve that purpose?
Was your outcome satisfactory – *did* you achieve your purpose?

We have deliberately made this a long activity. Normally, even though you will still want to be aware of all phases of the process and to review it as a whole, you will not conduct your review in such detail. The important thing is that you should regularly check your reading. What we have shown you is where and how to check. In carrying out your review you will need to check purpose specification, tactic and strategy choice and outcome and be aware of the part each plays in an effective overall approach to reading.

A personal programme of reading development

Effective reading to learn depends on orienting to the general aspects of the message in the text, sampling parts of the text for relevancy, selecting and reorganising items of meaning in the text, and checking understanding against purpose. These all involve skills which can be developed if they are not there, or there only in rudimentary form, and improved if they are there.

In developing the skills practice plays a major part. Obviously that is not something that we can help much on. We have seen the function of this book as being to increase your awareness of key components of reading to learn and to suggest techniques. It is something that you will have to take responsibility for yourself. But, then, the whole argument of this book is that reading is something you have to take full responsibility for. We have stressed in connection with almost every activity that the techniques we are suggesting can help up to a point but that beyond that point the process has to be transferred back 'into the head' and managed by the reader.

So it is with the long-term development of one's reading competence. It may be helpful, however, if we make some suggestions. First, what should we be aiming at? In a long-term programme of personal development with respect to reading to learn we should be trying to:

Purpose
1 define our reading purposes more adequately
2 build up a bank of specific reading purposes (Chapter 3)

Strategy
3 build up a personal repertoire of tactics and strategies
4 learn how to use them appropriately (Chapter 2)

106 *Reading to learn*

Outcome

5 develop our ability to assess the outcome of reading by checking outcome against purpose and against structure of text (Chapters 4, 5 and 6)

Review

6 develop our ability to appraise the effectiveness of 1–5 both separately and together.

A few words on each of these.

PURPOSE

The emphasis in Chapter 3 was on ways in which we could analyse purpose and so become more specific about it. Indeed, the approach may well have seemed analytically heavy. The emphasis in a development programme should be on building up a bank – in your head – of specific reading purposes so that when you are faced with some reading to learn you do not have to go through a cumbersome process of analysis and definition. It is still useful from time to time to use the full apparatus of purpose taxonomy and so on, but as you become more and more used to thinking about reading in terms of purpose you will find that purposes crystallise more readily. You will have an idea of the kind of purposes which might apply to a given passage and can short-circuit the whole procedure.

STRATEGY

The important thing here is to concentrate first on knowing when you are using a particular tactic and then on being able to adopt it when you want to and switch to and from it with ease. This will come fairly speedily. The second thing you have to work on is deciding what are the right tactics to employ. There is, of course, no one right strategy. Strategies will vary according to purpose and text and person. What you should be aiming for is increasing your command over tactics and strategy so that if one strategy does not work then you can try another. You are seeking to develop reading flexibility.

Becoming a competent reader: putting it together 107

OUTCOME

It is very easy to get slack about assessing outcome and so it is especially important to make use from time to time of techniques for achieving objectivity. They may be the straight comprehension-style answer or the rich 'structure of meaning', but the crucial thing is that they be used to secure honesty and precision in reporting outcome.

REVIEW

While this should be a feature, in however brief a form, of all reading to learn, from the point of view of development it is sensible to provide periodically for an extended and detailed review such as we worked through in the earlier part of this chapter. In such a review there is much to be said for using the whole battery of techniques – read record, flow diagram and the rest – because they introduce an element of objectivity into the process. Without them there are no checks on the accuracy of your subjective assessment. As a result of such an extended review you should be able to identify areas for particular development. You might feel you need to work more on outcome, for example, or on specifying purpose. The review essentially determines the shape of your overall programme – though some people like to plan a schedule ahead and work through it systematically, which is perfectly all right so long as it takes in the information provided by the periodic review.

Figure 7.2 presents in the form of an algorithm the points which such a periodic review might cover.

Answers (see page 101) Purposes for the 4 pieces

Piece 1 Recall of details – literal
Piece 2 Summary – interpretation
Piece 3 A critique – evaluation
Piece 4 Implications – extrapolations

108 *Reading to learn*

Figure 7.2 An algorithm for process-conversations with texts

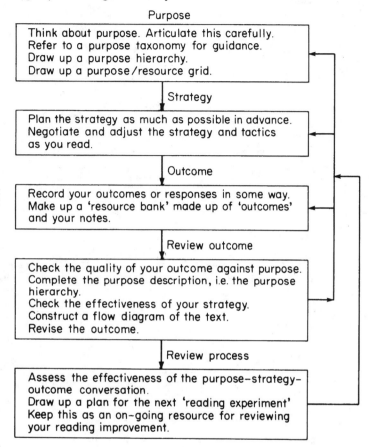

Epilogue
Notes for the tutor

This book is addressed directly to the reader. Our view is that the reader must take responsibility for improving his or her reading. Unless he or she does that it will not improve. But other people can help. As we said in our Foreword, we have had in mind in compiling this book the sort of study skill course for students that many universities and colleges are now beginning to provide. We have therefore, built in exercises which are best performed in pairs, and on various occasions we have indicated points at which group discussion might be profitable. Teachers can help, too. In many cases, group courses of the sort we are envisaging would be led by a group tutor. The following notes are intended to help anyone called on to assume such a role.

Unless the reader takes responsibility for his or her own reading it will not improve. It is absolutely imperative that the tutor should do nothing to weaken that assumption of responsibility. It follows that the tutor's role should be a complementary one. He should supplement the reader's own efforts, not replace them. There are, however, two very important things that he can provide: feedback and support.

The essence of our approach has been to provide the reader with feedback (information) about the way he or she reads, and so to help to bring a largely unconscious or subconscious process under more conscious control. For example, in Chapter 2 we explained how the reader could construct a record of the way a particular passage is read. By this means he or she could afterwards establish what reading tactics and strategies had been used and assess their appropriateness. Moreover, a little practice would enable the reader to get the feel of using a particular strategy, and thus to be able to

110   Reading to learn

choose deliberately to employ it. What was subconscious has now become at least in part conscious.

What the tutor can do is improve the quality of the feedback. For example, when the reader first produces a read, it may be hard to tell from the record exactly what kind of read it is. Fig. 2.2 shows five basic kinds of read and it is easy to see the difference between them. In practice, with a reader who is just starting to record reading, the record may be more ambiguous. Often, for example, the track appears to indicate something between kind (a) and kind (b): more hesitant than (a), more rapid than (b). Usually the ambiguity disappears after one or two goes, but initially the reader may like a little guidance in classifying the read. The tutor can point to the elements which push it one way or the other: the greater the number of hesitations the more it inclines to kind (b), for example. Very probably the reader will be saying things like: 'Well, for the first half it was pretty smooth and that's really kind (a), but then you slowed down and there were more hesitations, which makes it more like kind (b). Why do you think you changed? Were you aware that you were changing your approach?' The form of the tutor's remarks should be such as to push the onus back on to the reader to decide.

One advantage that the tutor has over the reader is experience. After having helped a few readers he or she will have seen far more reads than the reader has and so will be in a better position to decipher and identify them (though the reader should learn to identify independently).

The other thing that comes from experience is greater familiarity with the terms. The tutor will know what counts as a tactic and what as a strategy, what is a smooth read and what an item read and so on. This can be helpful in giving the group a sense of direction and forward movement. There is a lot of material to be absorbed and the momentum can be lost if too much time has to be spent at various stages in recalling what things are.

The tutor can help to preserve momentum in other ways, too. Some of the activities are complex and it is easy to get lost in less important detail. For example, in Activities 3.3 and 3.4 there are a number of different operations to be performed, as well as a fair bit of commentary and explanation. By organising the student's progression through the materials efficiently, the tutor can take the student's mind off that and help in focusing on the significant

Epilogue: Notes for the tutor 111

conceptual points. The tutor can distinguish what is organisational from what is conceptual from what is supplementary illustration and in this way reduce the information load on the student.

Where activities are long and complex it is best to break them down into phases, as we have tried to do in the text. We have also tried to break down techniques into fairly mechanical – sometimes even manual – operations. Listed out in such a way the scale of the operation may appear daunting. To the reader there seems so much information to absorb. Take, for example, our account of the 'structures of meaning' technique in Chapter 6. We set it out step by step so there seems a lot to take in. However, much of this is at a fairly low level (On separate sheets write . . . consider each cluster . . . lay out . . . etc.). The tutor can help the student by taking over responsibility for processing this low-level information, thus reducing the amount of attention he or she has to give it, and leaving the reader free to concentrate on the more conceptual side of self-monitoring.

Because our techniques are unfamiliar they may loom rather large. They are, however, only means to particular ends. By reminding the reader at each stage what the particular point of the operation is, the tutor can help the reader to get the techniques into proportion.

The techniques are complex, but then they are designed to do a very complex thing. They are intended to make external processes which are normally kept very internal. The techniques will do what they are supposed to do, but they cannot be skimped. They have to be taken slowly, thoroughly and systematically. They may, too, be engaging deep parts of the reader's personality. By the time we have reached maturity, reading is embedded in all kinds of experiences, emotional responses, beliefs about ourselves and attitudes to the world. The techniques are necessary but may be painful. They run up against all kinds of personal defences. For this reason the support that the tutor can give can be very valuable.

At various points in the text we provide examples of the way in which other readers have tackled particular operations (e.g. Jane in Chapter 3, Gareth in Chapter 5). Our purpose in providing these illustrations is firstly to show how the activity should be carried out, but, secondly, to provide an alternative perspective which might illuminate the reader's own approach. The tutor can help greatly in sharpening up the comparison and making it relevant to the reader.

Reading to learn

The tutor will find this easier if he has worked through the illustrative material beforehand.

Throughout the book we have laid great emphasis on 'talk-through'. Our aim is to develop the reader's capacity for talking himself or herself through a process introspectively. But, especially in the early stages, talk-through is aided by the tutor playing the part of the *alter ego*. The tutor should prompt not instruct; and here, as elsewhere, the more sympathetic the support the better.

Notes on chapters

CHAPTER 1

A good way to start the course is by group discussion. Ask people how they read. Answers will be unsystematic (see under heading 'Reading self-awareness'). Relate answers to 'preliminary vocabulary'. The aim is to start people thinking in terms of purpose, strategy, etc.

CHAPTER 2

It is more important here to get people producing their own read records than to start analysing them. Analysis should arise out of the read record. The reader's own patterns can then be related to our 'ideal types'. Work through Activity 2.2 slowly to let people get the hang of it. Once they have grown accustomed to the techniques they will be able to concentrate on themselves and their strategies.

CHAPTER 3

An important but abstract chapter. Take plenty of time, especially with Activities 3.1–3.3, which are designed more to get the reader thinking not so much to practise skills. Activity 3.4 comes later as a short-cut. Be content initially to develop a rough-and-ready purpose classification which you can refine as the course continues. Combine the activities with read recording (Ch. 2).

Epilogue: Notes for the tutor 113

CHAPTER 4

Scope for group discussion here (see commentary to activity 4.1).
The activities tend to be simpler and students enjoy them
(especially after grappling with purpose clarification). What is
require here is largely practice. Many activities lend themselves to
being done in pairs. Flow diagrams, for example, can be exchanged
and compared.

CHAPTER 5

A consolidating phase. Make sure the techniques are being used
correctly. Tutor's comments can be very valuable in confirming
and reinforcing points.

CHAPTER 6

The important thing is to develop the habit of checking read
against outcome. Registering a richer outcome is a bonus. Activity
6.2 is best treated as a kind of game. The tutor can assume a more
magisterial role in running the game. The students then don't have
to think about technique but can concentrate on checking outcome.

CHAPTER 7

The tutor should lie low. By this time the student should be able to
put it all together independently. The tutor may well have a
counselling role later when the student comes to thinking about a
personal programme for reading development.

The tutor might like to think in terms of establishing personal
programmes for reading development right from the start of the
course. The reader remains responsible for personal progress, but the
tutor provides counselling, feedback and support in the reader's
progression towards mutually agreed goals.